CRUCIAL QUESTIONS
IN APOLOGETICS

CRUCIAL
QUESTIONS
IN APOLOGETICS

Mark M. Hanna

BAKER BOOK HOUSE
Grand Rapids, Michigan 49506

Copyright 1981 by
Baker Book House Company

ISBN: 0-8010-4237-2

Library of Congress Catalog Card Number: 80-68768

Printed in the United States of America

To My Wife

with gratitude to God
for her sterling
exemplification
of
Proverbs 31:10-31

Contents

Preface

This volume has grown out of a series of lectures I delivered at Gordon-Conwell Seminary. I am indebted to Dr. Harold J. Ockenga, the long-time president of the seminary, and to Dr. William N. Kerr, then dean of the seminary, for their kind invitation that gave me the privilege of addressing one of the outstanding theological institutions in America.

I am also grateful to the faculty and students, whose warm response and pointed questions stimulated my thinking and prodded me to greater clarification of my position. The format of this volume reflects the dynamics of that interchange, for each of the lectures is followed by a section that sets forth their questions and my answers. This not only brings into focus the concerns of theological students as they encounter a novel—and sometimes iconoclastic—apologetic position, but it also serves to elucidate enigmatic and abstract parts of the lecture material.

Anti-intellectualism, which shuns critical consideration of the types of issues under discussion in this book, evidences few signs of waning among evangelicals. Thus the introduction has been

added to the original lectures to show the folly of such an attitude—especially as it stems from confusion about the nature and
function of philosophy.

Introduction

Although the touchstone of Christian apologetics must be the Bible, apologetics cannot dispense with philosophy. Indeed, if it attempts to do so, it will be the unwitting victim of bad philosophy. That is the nature of philosophy—and human thinking. The choice is never between philosophy and no philosophy; rather, it is always between good philosophy and bad philosophy.

Since the only use of the term *philosophy* in the Bible is a negative one (Col. 2:8), evangelical Christians have tended to view the entire enterprise of philosophical inquiry with suspicion—if not downright hostility. These are rather curious attitudes to take, however, for philosophy is not reducible to the Judeo-Gnostic speculations about which Paul warned the Colossian Christians.

Of course, there have been numerous metaphysical systems fabricated by philosophers that fall, in principle, under the Pauline censure. Any speculative claims, religious or philosophical, which conflict with the clear teaching of Scripture are properly repudiated (Isa. 8:20).

In this connection, the reductionistic and extreme strictures

11

of Logical Positivism have not been entirely devoid of value. They sounded the death knell of a long tradition in philosophy. Totalitarian and dogmatic attempts of speculative metaphysicians now appear to be relics of the past, having attained their consummate efflorescence in the ponderous and formidable system of Hegel.

This does not mean that speculative metaphysics is dead, or even moribund, for the synoptic vision of philosophers that impels them to fashion theoretical models of reality seems to be ineradicable—a rather "religious" impulse that resists complete and permanent suppression. Chastened metaphysicians now refrain from pontificating on the nature of reality in the grandiose style of a Plotinus, Spinoza, or Hegel. This new mood of caution and tentativeness will undoubtedly continue to condition future philosophical constructions.

Nevertheless, many contemporary philosophers have embraced intellectual perspectives that are hardly less inimical to the Christian faith. The various forms of linguistic and analytic philosophy, for example, tend toward fideism with respect to all metaphysical claims, whether philosophical or theological. If, as fideists assert, no one is able to escape the assumption of unjustifiable starting points for any theoretical system, then no claim to truth can overcome metaphysical relativism. Fideists not only hold that people may differ in the degree of their subjective assurance about metaphysical interpretations, they also maintain that such inner certitude can never be superseded by objective certainty. By its claim to be true, objective, and exclusive, the Christian faith is fundamentally incompatible with this widespread current in contemporary philosophy.

Unfortunately, a fideistic interpretation of the Christian faith seems to be increasing among evangelicals—partly because of the effect of recent developments in philosophy, and partly because such fideism seems to accord with tolerance and humility in a dangerously competitive world of clashing religious and ideological claims. To be sure, there have almost always been Christians who advocate fideism in the tradition of Tertullian and Kierkegaard, who gloried in the paradoxical and contended that "reason" precludes the exercise of faith, the *sine qua non* of authentic Christianity.

Apparently, for many Christians, antiphilosophy translates into antirationality. While it is true to say that the Bible must always be placed above reason, such a claim can be misunderstood and misused. For the assertion itself, which is derived from Scripture, is arrived at by a process of *reasoning* about the nature of the Bible and its relation to rationality. To create an antithesis between the Bible and reason is not only wrongheaded, but is also an egregious disservice to the Christian faith.

Reason should be understood as both reflective awareness and sound inference. Nothing in reason itself is anti-Christian. Indeed, reason is a gift from God and a component of the *imago Dei* (Gen. 1:26, 27). Moreover, reason is exemplified in Scripture— note the numerous instances of deduction and induction in the biblical text—and it is indispensable to the process of ascertaining what Scripture teaches.

Can there be saving faith without understanding, and can there be understanding without reason? Understanding too—despite the noetic effects of sin and the misemployment of reason— is a *sine qua non* of the Christian faith (Matt. 13:23). Perhaps this is also a way back to a qualified appreciation of philosophy.

As one examines what philosophers have been doing for 2500 years, he is able to discern certain abiding characteristics of the discipline. (1) Philosophy is philosophizing more than it is theoretical content. (2) Philosophy is marked by rigorous thinking in the pursuit of intellectual clarity. (3) Philosophy is critical in its argumentation and in its rational assessment of assumptions and truth claims. (4) Philosophy is centered in a quest for truth about crucial questions that perennially recur among reflective human beings. (5) Philosophy is not only analytic in its depth of insight but also synoptic in its breadth of vision.

It seems to me that we need more, not less, of that kind of intellectual rigor in our Christianity today. Is it not integral to loving God "with the mind"?

Opposition to "philosophy" continues, nevertheless. Why? In addition to the misconstrual of the nature of philosophy, there seem to be two main causes of this hostile sentiment among evangelicals. First, the assumption is widespread that philosophy is antithetical to divine revelation. It is true that philosophers generally engage in their tasks without an appeal to revelation. However, that no more entails the denial of revelation than the *methodological* naturalism of the empirical sciences entails the denial of supernaturalism. Some philosophers do not believe in revelation and some do, but there is no such thing as "philosophy"—unqualified and absolute—that precludes or even opposes revelation. Indeed, it is critical (philosophical) reasoning that has shown the gratuitousness of "philosophical" claims that revelation is impossible or untenable.

Second, the notion that philosophical inquiry militates against spiritual fervor is deep-rooted in evangelicalism. The annals of two thousand years of Christian history are replete with the casualties of philosophical subversion, not only in their forfeiture of biblical conviction but also in the erosion of their evangelistic zeal. There is more than one way to be spoiled by philosophy.

Scripture unequivocally teaches that our faith should not rest on the wisdom of men (I Cor. 2:4, 5), for no mere intellectual process is sufficient to produce genuine Christian conviction (Matt. 16:17; I Cor. 12:3). Nevertheless, cognitive statements and logical intelligibility are necessary for Christian faith (Rom. 10:9-17; I Cor. 15:1-4). The anti-intellectualism that fosters irrationality and fanaticism is no less reprehensible than the intellectualism that promotes pride and self-complacency. Christ ought to have preeminence in all things, our intellectual life included (Col. 1:18).

Science, not theology, is the main influence on the world of philosophy today. But theology still challenges philosophers to wrestle with the great questions of mankind. And philosophy has not abandoned its role as a gadfly that compels theologians to rethink their claims with more exacting scrutiny of their meaning, justification, and implications.

This volume is a response to key issues that are raised at the interface of theology and philosophy. As such, it seeks to chart a new course for evangelical apologetics in the future.

1
Crucial Challenges

The Contemporary Problem-Situation

Although apologetic issues were indirectly involved in my conversion to Christ, I, like Thomas in the twentieth chapter of the Gospel of John, had my severest struggle with doubt *after* I became a Christian.[1] For Thomas, the crisis was precipitated by the death of Christ. For me, it was brought on by the death of Christianity—that is, by what I thought was the irreversible loss of the objective knowledge that is the minimal requirement of Christianity's claim to be true.

In 1953, I went to the American University of Beirut to minister cross-culturally while I continued my undergraduate studies. There I met relentless critics of the Christian faith, both among the faculty and among fellow students. Two students who were majoring in philosophy sneered at my faith and imperiously affirmed, "If you take one course in philosophy, you'll give up Christianity." I took up the gauntlet, and somewhat to my surprise I

1. That Thomas was already a believer is indicated in John 13:10, 11.

found that my faith remained intact after the first course—and after considerably more exposure to philosophy beyond that.

As I continued to devour philosophical writings from the past and the present, I was faced with a painful dilemma. Should I allow the gradually developing schizophrenia in my mind to become a rigid and fixed compartmentalization with which I would resolve to live as a Christian, or should I seek intellectual integration under the control of an overarching principle?

My growing intellectual schizophrenia was fostered by the widely disparate nature, on the one hand, of mathematics, the empirical sciences, and to some extent, philosophy—the formerly fissiparous mother and currently parasitic handmaiden of the sciences—and on the other hand, the supernaturalistic claims of the Christian faith. The discrepancy seemed obvious and irremovable. In the former category were intellectual disciplines founded on the bedrock of objective, rational justification. In the other category was Christianity—indeed, all of the religions of the world and all speculative metaphysics—rooted, in the final analysis, in the arbitrariness of subjective, irrational assumption.

The toll exacted by this compartmentalization was too great, however, so I capitulated to the only alternative I could discern at the time. The inclusivistic, controlling principle that promised to restore intellectual wholeness was *faith*. If the ultimate points of reference for Christianity were faith postulates, I reasoned that it was no less the case that mathematics, the natural sciences, and philosophy were built on unprovable assumptions. Had not non-Euclidean geometries shown this with respect to mathematics, and had not Einstein's theory of relativity indicated this in the realm of the natural sciences? The foundations of philosophy were even more notoriously exposed as gratuitously based on faith than other disciplines. The subjectivization of philosophical starting points intensified from Descartes to Kant until all hope of recovering objectivity virtually disappeared. Even Hegel's metaphysical ingenuity failed to overcome Kant's limiting criticisms.

Was the Christian faith epistemologically dissimilar from other claims to "knowledge"? If every position is ultimately rooted in fideism (i.e., the postulation of unjustifiable starting points), why,

I asked myself, should the Christian faith be singled out as irrational or as intellectually unrespectable? Every perspective and every person seemed to be in the same predicament. It appeared to be a kind of delusion for one to think that he could break out of the fideistic circle. The intellectual priority of faith also seemed to be part of the spirit of the times. Barth, Brunner, Bultmann, and Tillich—to name only a few of the theological opinion-shapers of our era—had cogently contended for the primacy of faith. Even in evangelical circles there was no lack of fideistic protagonists.

But my repose in fideistic felicity proved to be short-lived. I found myself struggling for release from a quagmire of doubt and perplexity more profound and disconcerting than anything I had previously experienced.

Fideism seemed, *prima facie*, to comport perfectly with the priority of sovereign grace and the utter helplessness of sinful humanity. No one but God can savingly convict, convince, and convert a sinner. All human efforts to persuade by an appeal to rational norms appeared futile. Indeed, I reasoned, the latter are *themselves* based on faith-decisions that cannot be compelled.

In spite of this seemingly airtight case for fideism, its erosion in my intellectual development could not be forestalled. Although I shall elaborate on the untenability of fideism when I later assess the claims of presuppositionism,[2] two general observations can be made at this point.

First, every presentation of a case for fideism—in fact, the mere unargued *statement* of fideism—implicitly acknowledges rationality norms and their justificative decisiveness. In other words, any attempt to dispense with rationality or subordinate it to noncognitive faith is self-defeating. To state or imply that there are good reasons for holding fideism is, tacitly but inescapably, to deny fideism.

Second, fideism must be purchased at enormous cost. The price that one pays includes the loss of truth and knowledge, both

2. Although many writers use the term *presuppositionalism*, I prefer the shortened form.

theologically and nontheologically, *and the loss of the right to criticize.* Every claim reduces to an opinion. Every cognition dissolves into a belief. Every view, irrespective of its absurdities, is on the same epistemological footing with every other view. The demarcation between fact and fiction vanishes, and everyone finds refuge in the inviolable sanctity of his own experience and his own choice.

On that basis, then, anyone who claims that Christ is the truth, that the Bible is the Word of God, and that salvation is exclusively by grace through faith in Christ is both epistemologically benighted and theologically bigoted. Are we prepared to pay such a price? Rather, more to the point, can we pay such a price without betraying the Christian faith? Schleiermacher, Kant, Hegel, Bultmann, and Tillich (to mention some conspicuous examples from modern and recent thought) professed allegiance to the Christian faith while at the same time their epistemological assumptions served to undermine it. Did they not end with the husk of Christian terminology concealing the kernel of an alien philosophy? Can one be loyal to the Christian faith and, at the same time, empty it of objectivity, truth, and exclusivity? Can one be a fideist and avoid such a consequence?

Where can we go—we who are heirs of the Enlightenment, of Hume's skepticism, Kant's idealism, Lessing's "ugly ditch," Kierkegaard's radical subjectivity? Can we return to the naiveté of question-begging arguments for the existence of God and inductive "proofs" of the truthfulness of the Christian faith? This poses the fundamental problem for Christian apologists—in fact, not only for apologists but for every thinking Christian who reflects on the nature of Christian claims in a world of religious pluralism, skepticism, and secularism.

A brief sketch of recent philosophical developments will help us to comprehend the distinctive contours of our contemporary problem-situation. Any attempt to draw an intellectual map of the present scene must first of all recognize that the complexity and diversity of our times defy tidy classification. Nevertheless, making allowances for such extraordinary variety, we can discern certain formative influences and pervasive tendencies.

When Descartes responded to the skepticism of Montaigne, he set in motion not only a new school of thought—which we now refer to as Continental Rationalism—but also a new preoccupation of philosophers, whether Rationalists or non-Rationalists. Philosophical attention was turned inward. The focal concern of most philosophers from the seventeenth century until the twentieth century has been the *knowing self*. But the most influential subjectivization of knowledge was forged by Immanuel Kant in his *Critique of Pure Reason*. The *antimetaphysical principle* inherent in his epistemology has plagued theology to the present hour.

Hegel's system was the last great philosophical attempt to reinforce theological claims by an appeal to nontheological premises. Other attempts, most notably of Alfred North Whitehead, have shown that the intellectual impulse to establish such a relation did not disappear with the waning of Hegalianism. The *synthetic principle* exemplified in Hegelianism shows some signs of renewal today, although in considerably tempered form.

The *experiential principle* of Kierkegaardian and twentieth-century theological existentialism has not been alone in disavowing such reinforcement of theological claims. While existentialists tended to hold that theological assertions are irreducibly unique and *anti-* or *supra*rational, Logical Positivists invoked the *verifiability principle*. They argued that theological formulations, like metaphysical and ethical statements, are noncognitive, that is, neither true nor false. Accordingly, such assertions only express emotions or attitudes.

With the perspectival shift in Wittgenstein's mature thought (especially embodied in his work entitled *Philosophical Investigations*, in contradistinction to his much earlier *Tractatus*), his *usage principle* seemed to accommodate theological affirmations within a broadened understanding of the nature of meaning. Meaning, Wittgenstein contended, must not be restricted to Logical Positivism's reductionistic dualism of definitions and empirically-based claims. Wittgensteinians generally hold that theological assertions are part of a language game, and, as such, they have an interpersonal function that provides meaning to communicators who are participants in that game.

Karl Popper, one of our century's most influential philosophers of science, maintains that something more can be said about metaphysical and theological claims than that they are part of any number of diverse language games. Repudiating the verifiability principle, Popper maintains that the hypothetico-deductive nature of the empirical sciences exemplifies the epistemologically pivotal *principle of falsifiability*. This principle is not a criterion of meaning but of demarcation—distinguishing science from nonscience. However, science is the locus of "knowledge" about reality. By "knowledge" Popper means *doxa* (conjecture), not *episteme* (certainty), for *episteme* is unattainable. And by "reality" he means the intersection of "interpretation" and "data"—a notoriously unclear notion that is no less devastating to his epistemology than it was to Kant's. In any case, Popperian falsificationism views theological assertions as untestable assumptions which can only be held fideistically.

From the time of Immanuel Kant, for whom theological assertions were faith postulates, to Karl Popper, for whom theological claims are untestable hypotheses, the fideistic milieu for theology has become increasingly entrenched. Few theologians today contend that it is possible to argue successfully from philosophical or nontheological premises to theological conclusions.

Philosophy is widely thought to describe and analyze the "logic" of various disciplines and perspectives. By "logic" in this context is meant the special forms and usages of language, the particular meanings, assumptions, and inferences that characterize a demarcated area of inquiry or type of interpretation. The previously mentioned principles of Kantian antimetaphysics, Hegelian synthesis, Kierkegaardian experience, Positivistic verifiability, Wittgensteinian linguistic usage, and Popperian falsifiability have radically affected philosophy as well as theology.

Philosophy today is generally less ambitious, less dogmatic, less grandiose than it was fifty years ago. Although profound disagreements among philosophers concerning both method and content should not be glossed over, philosophy in the West is not widely considered a first-order discipline. Instead, it is viewed as a second-order discipline; its subject matter is not reality or the world but conceptual and linguistic analysis, especially as it investigates the nature, scope, and assumptions of various first-order disciplines, such as physics, biology, psychology, and so on.

The whittling away of philosophical pretensions has been salutary, in my judgment, but the excessively negative appraisal of philosophy not infrequently found among evangelicals is both gratuitous and unfortunate. It is gratuitous because such an appraisal is tacitly philosophical, and as such it becomes self-annihilating. It is unfortunate because philosophy, especially as a second-order discipline, is primarily a systematic approach to hard thinking, meticulous analysis, and sustained criticism. And evangelicals, no less than nonevangelicals, need to respect such rigorous discipline in all intellectual inquiry.

This admittedly sketchy and selective glance at some of the major philosophical determinants of our intellectual climate should aid us in understanding why we are facing the following pernicious but widely held assumptions today:

(1) It is doubtful that there is such a thing as truth; but if there is, it cannot be known.

(2) If there is such a thing as truth, it is very unlikely that there is any *religious* truth.

(3) Religious—or more appropriately, theological—formulations cannot be true because they are not cognitively meaningful.

(4) Physical phenomena have criteriological primacy with reference to knowledge claims.

(5) Since theological claims do not refer to physical phenomena—or, if they do, they also transcend them—there is no way to make them publicly adjudicable.

(6) If they are not publicly adjudicable, they cannot escape the liabilities of subjectivism.

(7) Whether or not theological terms and formulations refer to extrasubjective realities is at best problematic.

The crucial challenge distilled from these assumptions is as follows: since theistic arguments are unsound—or, in any case, if there is a sound one, it does not command anything near a consensus among philosophers—and since metaphysical claims cannot be established by historiography, even when it is granted that historiography can establish the historicity of any event, how is it possible to determine whether the object of our religious faith or theological claims is a real, extrasubjective, transcendent Being or merely a psychic projection whose ontological status is nothing more than that of Pegasus or a vivid dream?

How shall we tackle these seven ubiquitous assumptions—assumptions that are prevalent in Europe, North America, and Communist countries, but which are also leavening the rest of the world as westernization and urbanization[3] continue to transform cultures everywhere?

Never has the need been greater for ferreting out and assessing underlying presuppositions. As a former president of the American Scientific Affiliation wrote with admirable candor:

I went through ten years of post high school education, attended a seminary for another year, and taught for four more years in a Christian college before I even ran across the idea that my scientific (and personal) observations and conclusions were largely influenced by a set of non-sensory, philosophical presuppositions about the universe which I had accepted without question and without even giving them any thought. I hesitate to mention this naiveté but I take slight comfort in the knowledge that I was not alone. Too often, I have seen colleagues in psychology accept without question such "doctrines" as the irrelevance of religion, order in the universe, the non-existence of God, the superiority of the scientific method, the innate goodness of man, or determinism—to name a few. Most of the scientists that I know avoid philosophy like the plague yet their whole work is based on the acceptance of philosophical assumptions that they neither perceive nor care about.[4]

---

3. In this century we are witnessing a shift from 13 percent of the world's people living in cities in the year 1900 to a projected 87 percent in urban centers in the year 2000.
4. Gary R. Collins, "A Word From the President," *American Scientific Affiliation Bulletin* (April 1974).

While it is difficult to overestimate the importance of exposing presuppositions, a caveat is urgently needed at this point. The pervasiveness of assumptions does not warrant the leap to *presuppositionism*, the reduction of all knowledge claims to fideistic postulates. Although philosophy cannot independently provide or prove basic theological claims, it may show that revelation is possible and it may establish and undergird certain nonrevelational truth-claims that comport with Christian affirmations. Philosophy can also explicitate universal principles which have corroborative relevance to Christian claims (as I seek to show later in connection with "veridicalism," a new apologetic approach which I propose as the alternative to the impasse created by incompatible traditional views). A good apologist must engage in presuppositional analysis and assessment, but if he acquiesces to presuppositionism, his intellectual labor becomes nothing more than a futile charade.

An apologist's prosecution of presuppositional analysis and criticism should operate on four major levels: the popular, the academic, the religious, and the philosophical. In the West, especially in North America, the popular level is characterized by a pluralism that runs the gamut from crass superstition to dogmatic scientism. In spite of multifarious subcultures, there is a diffuse ethos whose chief motif is materialistic hedonism—although it is partially concealed by a veneer of religious and altruistic interests. The pragmatic principle of *workability* reigns supreme as the arbiter of truth and value. And the determination that something "works" is made in reference to the ends of technological efficiency and psychological and physical pleasure.

Although the academic level is transcultural in a way that the popular level is not, its center of gravity is in Europe and North America. It shares some of the salient features of the popular ethos in whose diverse cultural soils it is planted, but it also has its distinctive emphases. It is generally less naive in its tendency toward scientism, but it is predominantly secularistic and humanistic nonetheless. Its attitude of wariness toward the natural sciences stems from a greater perception of the limitations and failures of the sciences since the turn of the century. Its misgivings about science and technology notwithstanding, academia over-rates the authority and promise of both.

With the exception of a small minority, academic communities are philosophically unsophisticated. Consequently, they are characterized by relative indifference toward critical questions about the epistemological foundations of their intellectual disciplines and their world views. Preoccupation with manipulative skills in their respective disciplines, even on the most abstract levels, tends to crowd out sustained and rigorous scrutiny of underlying principles and ultimate truth-claims. On the popular level, serious interest in theological questions is often precipitated by a threat to personal well-being; on the academic level, earnest inquiry into theological concerns is rarely evoked by any circumstance.

The religious level is prodigiously variegated. Nevertheless, most of the religions and cults of the world have sufficiently distinct beliefs and practices to enable apologists to ascertain the communicative adjustments that are needed for an effective presentation of the gospel. Applied apologetics must be tailored for each cult and each religion no less than it must seek to relate to the distinctive contours of the popular level in a given culture or subculture and of the academic level in its quasiuniversal character.

Apologetics finds its most formidable task, however, on the philosophical level. It is here that it does its profoundest work as an intellectual discipline. We find this sphere of the human activity of philosophy (disregarding what is misleadingly called Eastern philosophy) riddled with an avowed and self-conscious ontological naturalism, that is, a view of reality that is essentially antisupernatural. With relatively few exceptions, the philosophical world is either apathetic or antipathetic in its attitude toward the Christian faith. But among those who take a vital interest in it—pro or con—there are four overarching issues debated today. I designate these the intelligibility challenge, the falsifiability challenge, the translatability challenge, and the justifiability challenge.

(1) The intelligibility challenge is the contention that the basic terms of the Christian faith are incoherent. One cannot justifiably believe in God, because the concept "God" embraces logical in-

compatibilities. If one cannot make that concept logically clear, he is not entitled to affirm that there is an independent reality which is characterized by the attributes ascribed to him by Christians. Believing in God makes as much sense as believing in square circles.

(2) The falsifiability challenge maintains that Christian claims cannot be true because there must be something these claims affirm about the world that would not be the case if they are false. In what respect would the world be different if Christianity were false? For example, would any state of affairs serve to falsify or make unreasonable the claim that there is an all-knowing, personal God who is both perfectly loving and omnipotent? If nothing can be specified as a potential falsifier, then the claim says nothing informative, and it cannot legitimately be said to be true or false.

(3) The translatability challenge is a philosophical sibling of the falsifiability challenge. It insists, however, that theological statements are devoid of cognitive significance because they purport to refer to a reality that transcends the empirical world. Since we can only have cognitive access to *empirical* referents, theological assertions remain informationally vacuous unless they can be translated into, or be made equivalent to, statements about empirical states of affairs.

(4) The justifiability challenge argues that even if Christianity's basic theological concepts are intelligible and its central theological affirmations are cognitive, they are not rationally credible. Theistic arguments are unsound and empirical data (including historical traces and religious experience) are inconclusive. Since there is no way to justify its constitutive claims, it is arbitrary, if not irrational, to hold the Christian faith to be true.

These four challenges are contemporary philosophy's most formidable attacks on Christian knowledge claims. They are the most formidable because they are made on the basis of *epistemological objectivism*, the view that there are extrasubjective states of affairs, true and false propositions, sound and unsound arguments, objective knowledge, and universal and necessary canons of rationality.

Other criticisms of the Christian faith which repudiate epistemological objectivism cannot logically be taken with seriousness. It is of paramount importance for us to see why this is the
case. Nothing is more absurd than the attempt to assert or argue
for radical epistemological relativism or subjectivism. And nothing is more ludicrous than to attack the Christian faith from such
a stance. For either human thinking is characterized by a capacity
for apprehending objective realities and timeless principles or it
is a process whose sequential events are determined by nonrational causes. If it is the latter, it is incapable of knowing anything—even that it is in fact so determined. Relativity to
nonrational causes is either known nonrelatively or it is not known
at all. But if it is known nonrelatively, then relativism is false.

Whether the relativist makes physical, psychological, cultural,
or any other nonrational causes totally determinative of reasoning,
he also makes it impossible to know this itself. Since such relativism is asserted to be true objectively, it is self-nullifying. If
consciousness and reason are reducible to physical events and
bodily behavior, as materialistic naturalists claim, then all of our
thinking is simply the result of blind forces. Nothing can be known
to be true or false, and believing one proposition rather than
another, even its contradictory, could never be justified. And this
means that naturalism itself can never be justified. Thus, there
is no reason why one should hold it any more than he should
hold its contradictory. Such claims, therefore, are self-defeating.
Both truth and value are precluded in principle by radical subjectivism and can only be professed and pursued by self-
deception among its doctrinaire enthusiasts.

All attempted critiques of the Christian faith on the basis of
subjectivism, relativism, and reductive naturalism are ineffective
because they are incoherent. Since they cannot make their own
position logically intelligible, advocates of these bizarre theories
have nothing with which to oppose Christianity.

Although the Christian faith, for these reasons, is logically
immune from criticism coming from such sources, it is incum-
bent upon apologists to show this and to explain why that is the
case. This task, among others, is an indispensable component in

our obedience to the biblical injunction "to give an answer to everyone who asks you to give the reason for the hope that you have" (I Peter 3:15). Only God can prepare us to do so; only God can supply the divine weapons that have power to tear down strongholds, and to demolish arguments and every pretension that sets itself up against the knowledge of God, and to take captive every thought to make it obedient to Christ (II Cor. 10:4, 5).

Questions and Answers

Question 1

"How are we to understand the possibility of severe doubt in the life of a Christian—such as Thomas? Since a regenerated believer in Christ has a new nature and the Holy Spirit, how can he fall victim to doubt about that which is the foundation of his faith and experience?"

Answer: In case this question challenges the claim that Thomas was a genuine believer prior to his sensory encounter with the resurrected Christ, I want to emphasize the statement that Christ made in John 13:10, 11. It is clear that Thomas was with the disciples in John 13 (cf. John 14:5). Christ also indicated that all of the disciples were spiritually cleansed except Judas Iscariot (John 13:11; cf. Titus 3:5). Hence, it is incontrovertible that a genuine Christian believer may experience deep doubt.

Was Thomas a special case, however? That is, does he represent certain possibilities that cannot obtain after the new era in which believers are indwelt by the Holy Spirit? Apart from other recorded instances of severe doubt among believers (e.g., Matt. 11:2-6), post-Pentecost Christians seem to be susceptible to similar skeptical crises. One of the ministries of the Holy Spirit is to produce assurance (Rom. 8:16). If He is grieved (Eph. 4:30), and if a believer is not filled with the Spirit (Eph. 5:18), such assurance will not be the experience of a believer. II Peter 1:9 seems to imply that a genuine Christian may lack assurance or be plunged into a state of doubt.

Of course, there are many degrees and types of doubt. And there are many causes as well. Thomas and the early disciples were in special circumstances—without the benefit of all that was subsequently revealed and that constitutes the New Testament. They did not understand the sequence of events as the Old Testament had foretold them (cf. Luke 24:25-27). Confusion and disillusionment raised profound questions in the mind of Thomas, who was left without the faith-confirming experience the other disciples had when Christ presented himself to them bodily in the upper room.

A genuine Christian may fall into doubt for a variety of reasons—or due to any number of causes. A neglect of Scripture reading, or of prayer, or of Christian fellowship may predispose one in that direction. A persuasive intellectual attack on the Christian faith may precipitate a crisis of doubt. It may also come from a tragedy—the loss of a loved one, or of one's health. Since it is not possible for the elect to be permanently taken captive by deception (Matt. 24:24), a believer's experience of doubt has divinely appointed limits and will not issue in the settled repudiation of the Christian faith. A Christian may call the foundations of his faith into question for a time, but it is likely that he will remain in such a state for a relatively short period, for it is displeasing to God who is his faithful, chastening heavenly Father (Heb. 11:6; 12:6).

Since severe doubt in the mind of the genuine Christian is a possibility, every believer ought to maintain the kind of spiritual, moral, and intellectual life that will preclude its emergence. In academic circles intellectual challenges to the Christian faith are hardly avoidable, but an adequate knowledge of the Scriptures and effective counterarguments can avail to overthrow such attacks. But since the chief source of doubt is a supernatural adversary, nothing less than the whole armor of God will suffice (Gen. 3:1-5; Luke 8:12; Eph. 6:10-18).

Question 2
"Why do you claim that objective knowledge is essential to Christianity?"

Answer: An informed understanding of epistemology, which is that branch of philosophy that studies the nature, scope, and limits of human knowledge, leads to the conclusion that objective knowledge is inescapable—not only for Christianity but in general. By "objective knowledge" is meant the givenness of various states of affairs and of the truth or falsity of propositions, irrespective of the acceptance or nonacceptance of them by human subjects.

"States of affairs" is a term that refers to anything that is or is not the case—for example, the presence of the San Andreas fault in California, the typewriter on my desk, the inanimate nature of the typewriter, and so forth. A "proposition" is the meaning of a statement that declares that something is or is not the case. Every such meaning is either true or false, and its truth or falsity is determined by the state of affairs to which it refers. If the state of affairs is as the proposition asserts it to be, the proposition is true; if it is not, the proposition is false.

The Christian faith consists of more than propositions, but if the truth-value (the truth or falsity) of the propositions which define it is claimed to be determined by something other than the states of affairs to which they refer, then the Christian faith is not what it purports to be. That is, it purports to be the truth about actual states of affairs—not about something that is fictional or arbitrary. Objective knowledge is essential to the Christian faith because Christianity claims to be the truth about the nature of reality. If reality does not have a determinate structure and if propositions are not timelessly true, then the Christian faith is not what it claims to be. Without the doctrines (propositions) of the Trinity, the incarnation of the Son of God, the redeeming death of Christ, the bodily resurrection, the sinfulness of human beings, and so on, the historic Christian faith is not definable. To interpret these doctrines as circumlocutions for something other than straightforward reference to actual states of affairs—metaphysical or historical, as the case may be—is to repudiate that historic faith.

The very nature of the Christian faith, therefore, is predicated on epistemological objectivism, which I have delineated toward the end of the preceding chapter as "the view that there are extra-subjective states of affairs, true and false propositions, sound and unsound arguments, objective knowledge, and universal and necessary canons of rationality." Just as there are definitive ontological claims made by the Christian faith, so there are explicit epistemological consequences entailed by it—and objective knowledge is one of them. All attempts to argue otherwise exhibit serious misunderstanding of either the Christian faith or of the nature of knowledge—or of both.

Question 3

"You have recounted something of the threat posed to your faith by philosophy. What is it that makes philosophy inimical to the Christian faith?"

Answer: The question seems to presuppose that "philosophy" is both monolithic and antagonistic to the Christian faith. There are many different philosophies and philosophers. Some of them are incompatible with or opposed to the Christian faith and others are not. However, if "philosophy" is understood primarily in its formal sense, that is, as the rational, critical assessment of basic human beliefs, the Christian faith is not only unthreatened but actually served by philosophy. Christians have nothing to fear by the application of rational criticism to the evaluation of any sphere of life or inquiry. It was due to inexperience and naiveté that I once thought that a great deal of higher education—particularly philosophy—was antithetical to the Christian faith. A Christian ought to realize, however, that reason and education are allies and that the pursuit of excellence in the multiform areas of human inquiry can be God-glorifying.

On the other hand, in deference to an important element of truth in the question, more needs to be said about this presumed threat. Since some influential philosophers (for example, the late Bertrand Russell) have been outspokenly antagonistic to the Christian faith, it is understandable that inadequately informed Christians (and non-Christians) have the impression that "philosophy" is inimical to Christianity. Such a conclusion is clearly unjustified.

Although it is true that philosophy characteristically disavows dependence upon divine revelation, opposition to divine revelation is not entailed by philosophical methodology in this basic sense of the term. Although a philosopher engages in his discipline on the basis of reason, he may be a believer in divine revelation or he may not be a believer. If he is not a believer, he may be open or closed to the possibility of divine revelation. If he is closed to the possibility, this indicates something about his particular presuppositions or attitude rather than anything about the nature of philosophy *per se*. For philosophy, in the formal generic sense, has never been shown to nullify the possibility of divine revelation.

In view of the apparent philosophical claim to the sufficiency of unaided reason, it is not surprising that some Christians consider philosophy to be at variance with their faith. What they should be apprised of, however, is that "philosophy" entails no such claim and is, therefore, not an adversary. Only specific philosophical perspectives or particular presuppositions are antagonistic to the Christian faith. In view of Christianity's recognition of the theological roots of formal reason—namely, the divinely created *imago Dei*—the function of philosophy that applies it in cautious, critical assessment of beliefs is to be welcomed as a genuine ally.

Question 4

"Would you elaborate on the nature of the scientific and philosophical developments that once led you—and seem to lead many today—to a fideistic interpretation of all views in general and Christianity in particular?"

Answer: For most people who embrace fideism or skepticism, the route is probably something like the following. In the initial stages of their education, they make no clear differentiation between the credibility of the religious beliefs they are taught and the rest of the pronouncements they encounter in their education. As they grow in years and maturity, they begin to distinguish them on the assumption that religious beliefs rely on unprovable faith and scientific claims rely on reason and evidence. Some people retain this view all of their lives—either fideistically accepting or skeptically rejecting the religious faith. Those who proceed with their education to an advanced understanding of the sciences—and especially the philosophy of science—invariably leave their naive credulousness toward the sciences behind.

With a new understanding of the pervasiveness of presuppositions and the influence of nonscientific considerations—such as "elegance," "symmetry," "beauty," and the like—one can no longer maintain a clear line of demarcation between the subjective and objective with reference to the sciences. And, therefore, "objectivity" is no longer seen as the unequivocal hallmark of the sciences in contradistinction to the "subjectivity" of religious faith.

One readily finds support—specious as it is—for this overarching principle of faith, which is now embraced as the epistemological ultimate for the whole of human "knowledge." The history of the sciences is replete with refutation, revision, and revolution. Nothing can be considered absolute and inviolable—not even in the most empirical sciences. What then can be said of those that are semi-empirical (e.g., the behavioral sciences) and nonempirical (e.g., logic and mathematics)?

Hypothetical interpretation seems to be the basis for all the sciences. But that is simply synonymous with "faith." Mathematics appears to be reducible to uninformative definition and ordered axiomatization. That, too, seems to be another way of saying that the whole of mathematics is based on faith. Religious and philosophical views are notoriously diverse, relativized by time, place, culture, and idiosyncrasy. The entirety of human "knowledge," then, is directly or indirectly conjectural—that is, it is either straightforward assumption or inference based on assumption. Every attempt to argue that it is not leads to ultimate starting points that are unjustifiable—which is another way of saying that they are faith postulates. Hence, the totality of what is misleadingly called "human knowledge" is, in reality, a tissue of variegated belief.

With the espousal of such fideism, one tends to look with contempt on the naive unsophisticates who think that there is a difference between knowledge and faith. No less is he inclined to scorn those who claim that their views are the exclusive truth— despite the inconsistency implied in his attitude.

Not only have scientific revolutions (e.g., Einsteinian versus Newtonian physics), mathematical inadequacies (e.g., Riemannian versus Euclidean geometry), and philosophical failures (e.g., Hegelianism, Logical Positivism) undermined confidence in knowledge claims, but recent theological perspectives have also abetted the attack on certainty. When Barth and Brunner—and a host of other existential theologians—contend that if we can have *knowledge* of God then we cannot *believe* in God, faith postulation is made the highest virtue and the final point of reference. Accordingly, faith alone preserves the subjective decision that is essential to human dignity. Knowledge is not only incompatible with doubt, but it also precludes faith. For faith cannot operate without doubt. Indeed, doubt pervades the whole of human life, and without the faith decision that is made against the background of doubt and in spite of doubt, authentic human existence cannot be realized.

It thus appears that every area of human inquiry converges at the same point. In the final analysis, all of our "knowledge" is interpretation, and all of our interpretation consists of faith postulates.

The foregoing scenario describes that which essentially led me—and I believe, leads many—to fideism. It has the appearance of humility, for all of us are limited by the same principle, thereby leaving no room for boasting. It also seems to be the most honest position, for all of us must admit that we cannot justify our starting points. All of these virtues are specious, however, for fideism is self-defeating. As long as its self-annihilating inconsistency is not understood, it will appear attractive and convincing, especially to those who prize humility, wisdom, and honesty.

Question 5
"Would you clarify your claim that 'the mere unargued statement of fideism' tacitly denies fideism?"

Answer: Fideism, in the comprehensive sense in which the term is being used here, denotes the view that *all* claims are faith postulates or are based on such gratuitous assumptions. Accordingly, logic and science, no less than philosophy and theology, are ultimately unjustifiable. No rationality norm can be justified without circularity, and consequently it cannot be truly justified. Even the usefulness of such disciplines or norms cannot serve to justify them. For this principle of pragmatism needs justification itself. And even if it could be "justified" by appealing to some other principle, that in turn would need justification. Either one calls a halt at some point or concedes an infinite regress. In the former case, arbitrariness is patent. Why call a halt at any particular point in the purportedly justificative process? In the case of an infinite regress, justification is just as elusive, for conceding an infinite regress is an admission that no genuinely justificative criterion can be found.

In the articulation of the fideistic position, which the foregoing paragraph sets before us, one can discern several incoherencies. First, the mere expression of the meaning of fideism appeals to the principle of noncontradiction (i.e., that a proposition cannot be both true and not true). The appeal is to an absolute principle, for not only fideism but every position and every claim would be unintelligible without it. The meaning of fideism, the possibility of its truth-value, and its distinguishability from anything else, all depend upon the absoluteness of the principle of noncontradiction. And that principle cannot be postulated or assumed to be true or criteriological, for without the nonpostulational knowledge of the principle prior to every act of postulation, there could be no postulation. And without postulation, there can be no fideism.

To elucidate this further, if one says that he will *assume* the principle of noncontradiction and only after that proceed to use it, he puts himself in an impossible position. The reference to his own identity ("I will assume . . .") and the proposition which is to be assumed ("the principle of noncontradiction") cannot even be reflectively entertained unless the principle of noncontradiction is already implicitly grasped and applied. Therefore, the principle can never be assumed, for it must always be known *prior* to every act of assumption. The linguistic or symbolic *expression* of the principle is something that may be done after the cognition, tacit or explicit, of the principle, but the implicit apprehension of the principle cannot be preceded by any intellectual act of postulation.

Although there are states of affairs that obtain and are known or knowable besides the principle of noncontradiction, all that is required for fideism to be exposed as false is the adduction of this one counterinstance. That is, the nonpostulational givenness of the principle of noncontradiction provides a clear case of a counter-example to the principle of *universal* postulation insisted upon by fideism. All that is required for a universal proposition (one which has the form, "All A's are B's") to be shown to be false is the adduction of one true particular proposition that is its con-tradictory. Since it is true that at least one proposition (the prin-ciple of noncontradiction) *cannot* be postulated, it follows that it is false that all propositions are or can be postulated. And since fideism requires the nonpostulation of the principle of noncon-tradiction, fideism—which asserts that all propositions are pos-tulated—is false. By thus showing how fideism reduces to absurdity, one is able to understand how the mere unargued state-ment of fideism tacitly denies fideism.

Question 6
"Why can't criticism continue within the framework of fideism? Can't people criticize each other's views on the basis of criteria that are not claimed to be any more than opinions?"

Answer: The answer to this query is contained in the response to question 5. Since fideism cannot achieve self-consistent identity, it provides no framework in which criticism—or for that matter, anything—can take place. In reality, fideism is a nonposition; the term *fideism* lacks a referent that can actually obtain because it is devoid of the minimal conditions of intelligibility.

Since the aim of criticism is to ascertain meaning and truth-value, nonpostulational criteria must be invoked. Merely to say that all criteria are postulated does not make them postulations. One can designate the principle of noncontradiction a "postulation," but that does not transmute it into a postulation. Its status is something quite different, as we have seen. It can only be a *given* and nothing else.

If nothing but opinions could be appealed to as criteria, genuine criticism could not be achieved, nor could the purpose of criticism be realized. Its chief objective is the rational justification and refutation of various truth claims. If every claim reduces to opinion, no such achievement is possible and the entire process of criticism is reduced to an exercise in futility. Furthermore, if one claims that all criteria are opinions, or if he claims that he does not know whether they are or are not opinions, he contradicts his professed fideism. Even if he merely opines that they are all opinions, he reflectively knows that he opines and that he does not dogmatize, and he thereby contravenes fideism.

The attempt to formulate a theory of fideism is predicated upon knowledge, that is, upon that which is nonfideistic. No such attempt can succeed, for the purported theory can never attain logical intelligibility. No more can criticism ever achieve integrity if it is attempted without a frame of reference constituted by nonpostulated criteria.

Question 7
"Why can't one *nondogmatically* claim that Christ is the truth, that the Bible is the Word of God, and that salvation is by grace through faith in the gospel of Christ

without being epistemologically benighted and theologically bigoted?"

Answer: Whether or not one is a fideist, if he claims that one *ought* to accept these theological doctrines, he cannot avoid the implication that there are *reasons* why one ought to do so. But if one is a fideist, his claim that Christ is the truth is a sham. For him there can be no truth—at least no knowable truth. Even predicating truth of Christ is an assertion that he has no right to make. If a fideist says, "I believe that Christ is the truth," he must face the question, "Why do you believe that Christ is the truth and not Buddha or Muhammad, or someone else—or no one?" Is it not the fideist who is theologically bigoted? For unlike non-fideists, he cannot make the claim on the basis of supporting reasons.

Furthermore, whether one makes a theological or nontheological claim, it is the combination of gratuitousness and intolerance that most egregiously constitutes bigotry. In fact, a fideist is a prime candidate for bigotry, because by definition fideism is adherence to a belief without reasons. On the other hand, a non-fideist may "dogmatically" (i.e., exclusively and assuredly) claim that Christ is the truth without being bigoted. Bigotry involves both objective and subjective factors, notably the absence of reasons and the presence of an attitude of contempt and intolerance toward others.

A fideist is also epistemologically benighted because he fails to understand the implications about knowledge that such theological claims—indeed, any claims—have. To assert that "Christ is the truth" is to make an unintelligible sound unless some things are *known*. What it is that one is doing (asserting rather than questioning) and what it is that one is asserting (the meaning of the individual terms and of the entire statement) cannot be grasped without conformity to conditions of intelligibility (noncontradiction, referentiality, etc.). Since a fideist denies the givenness of the conditions of intelligibility (although he tacitly acknowledges them in the act of denying them), inevitably he is epistemologically benighted.

Question 8
"Isn't your claim that the Christian faith is objective, true, and exclusive incompatible with faith? Shouldn't faith stop short of such claims?"

Answer: The critical issue is the meaning of faith. If faith is defined as assumption without justification (i.e., postulation), then it is patently incompatible with such a claim. For a claim of objectivity, truth, and exclusiveness implies the availability of justification.

The term *faith* is not used in the Bible to mean postulation, however. Genuine faith means more than merely believing that something is or is not the case. It is basically trust or reliance. Such trust must be based on knowledge—by means of universal (Rom. 1:18-20) or special revelation (John 14:9; II Tim. 3:15). The apostle Paul said that he walked by *faith* (II Cor. 5:7) and he also said, "I *know* whom I have believed" (II Tim. 1:12). Properly understood within their biblical context, faith and knowledge are compatible. Indeed, in man's relationship with God they are incomplete without one another.

The consistent teaching of Scripture is that the Christian faith is objective, true, and exclusive. And yet the Bible promotes faith. In fact, it does so on that very basis. A Christian should take his cue from the Scriptures, therefore, and not stop short of such claims in the name of "faith." For any conception of faith that severs it from its objective, epistemological base is at variance with biblical teaching.

Question 9
"Why do you dismiss theistic arguments as question-begging, and inductive proofs of the Christian faith as naive? Aren't there capable philosophers and theologians who make use of such arguments?"

Answer: There certainly are competent philosophers and theologians who accept one or more theistic arguments as sound and employ inductive evidence for the justification of the Christian faith. In philosophy, consensus is generally more important than the competence of an individual thinker. Of course, neither one guarantees the truth of a given claim.

To understand why they are problematic at best, one should consider the philosophical arguments leveled against them. Even those philosophers who hold to one of the arguments generally repudiate the others. The primary weakness of theistic arguments lies in their unwarranted assumptions about the nature of reality and the relationship of human thinking to ultimate reality.

For example, does causality—or causality as we know it— extend beyond the world of space and time? Does the necessity that characterizes logical relations or our thought processes apply to extralogical or extraconceptual reality? Do key terms have clear definitions? Do they shift their meaning from premises to conclusion (for example, the term *exists* in an argument that because the world exists . . . God exists). In my judgment, advocates of theistic arguments have yet to succeed in defending their positions against devastating criticisms. For a more extensive discussion of theistic arguments and inductive evidence, see my forthcoming book, *Metapologetics: Can the Christian Faith be Justified?*

Question 10
"What was the skeptical challenge of Montaigne, and how did Descartes respond to it?"

Answer: Michel Eyquem de Montaigne (1533-1592) was deeply influenced by the skepticism of Sextus Empiricus (second to third century), who had adopted the views of the radical skeptic, Pyrrho (c. 360-270 B.C.). In an essay entitled, "Apology for Raimond Sebond," Montaigne ostensibly defended the thesis of the fifteenth-century Spanish theologian who argued that reason alone could establish the doctrines of the Christian faith. By exposing the limitations and fallacies of sense experience and reason, Montaigne contended that since they could not apprehend reality or provide knowledge, religious tenets must be based on faith alone. Since no reasoning is reliable, wrote Montaigne, Sebond's inadequate reasons were not to be faulted. They are as good or as bad as anyone else's reasons. Besides, only the grace of God can bring one to the truth about God and to genuine conversion.

The three major currents of a rediscovered Pyrrhonism, an antireligious Renaissance, and a formidable Reformation found expression in Montaigne's essay. By this convergence, philosophers and theologians of the late sixteenth and early seventeenth centuries were confronted with a severe intellectual crisis. Herbert of Cherbury, Francis Bacon, and René Descartes were especially concerned to find a sound basis for knowledge that would overcome the profound skeptical assaults of Montaigne.

Descartes was convinced that certainty was attainable, and that the chief problem was the fashioning of a method by which knowledge could be established. His answer to Montaigne's challenge found its focus in a fourfold method for removing doubt. This consisted of (1) accepting only that which was clear and distinct; (2) dividing difficulties into as many parts as possible; (3) reflecting in an orderly fashion, beginning with the simple and proceeding to the complex; and (4) enumerating and reviewing to insure that nothing had been omitted. On that basis, Descartes contended that universal skepticism is obviated by the indubitability of one's own existence. On the presupposition, "in order to think, it is necessary to exist," he found his existence clear and distinct, and therefore certain. Doubting and being deceived are species of thinking, and they necessitate the existence of a thinking being.

Descartes then proceeded to argue for knowledge of extra-mental objects by invoking the existence of God. This he believed he could prove on the grounds that God's actual existence alone can account for the idea of a perfect and infinite Being which is found among the data of consciousness. On this basis the rest of our knowledge can be guaranteed—if we are careful to assent only to that which meets the standards of the fourfold method for eliminating doubt.

Descartes's restriction of his starting point to the data of consciousness and his epistemological appeal to God led to enormous difficulties in the subsequent history of philosophy. Given his starting point, there seemed to be no way to bridge the Cartesian gap between consciousness and extrasubjective reality. Moreover, his arguments for the existence of a perfect and infinite Being were criticized as question-begging and circular. In spite of Descartes's determined quest for certainty, various forms of skepticism have appeared again and again in subsequent centuries—and a strong current persists in philosophical circles to this day.

Question 11
"What was Kant's antimetaphysical principle and how has it plagued theology to the present?"

Answer: Immanuel Kant (1724-1804) created a synthesis of Rationalism and Empiricism that is epitomized in his dictum, "Concepts without percepts are empty; percepts without concepts are blind." He argued that "knowledge" is possible only because the subjective conditions of our minds serve to organize raw data into phenomena. Accordingly, since that which transcends space and time is not accessible to sensory perception, speculative metaphysics (most notably theistic proof) is unattainable.

Since I hold no brief for theistic arguments—at least in the classical sense—I do not deplore the mere fact of Kant's opposition to speculative metaphysics. It is another facet of his antimetaphysical stance to which I object, namely, his *a priori* nullification of the possibility of divine revelation. Propositional revelation in the form of the Scriptures constitutes metaphysical knowledge, which was anathema to Kant. Cognitive awareness of God (Rom. 1:18-20), who transcends space and time, was deemed impossible under the restrictions of Kantian epistemology. Divine revelation in the incarnation of the Son of God was also precluded.

All religions, including Christianity, were reduced by Kant to morality. The two essential religious doctrines, the existence of God and a future life, he justified as faith-postulates based on moral experience. Kant's antimetaphysical principle is an implication of his epistemology, and it is most pernicious in its denial that man can possess any genuine knowledge of God by general or special revelation.

Much theology has been adversely affected by this principle in its opposition to the biblical claim that God has revealed himself and his will in the form of words and meanings. Its negative influence is also seen in the mysticism (Schleiermacher), ethicism (Ritschl), and experientialism (Otto) that have characterized the views of some thinkers, and in fideism, most conspicuously seen in "dialectical theologians," such as Kierkegaard, Barth, Brunner, Bultmann, *et al.* Radical conclusions were drawn on the basis of Kant's idealism and Kierkegaard's existentialism, including his stress on "the infinite qualitative distinction between time and eternity." With the assumption that an unbridgeable chasm separates appearance and reality, extreme theological skepticism and irrationalism became inevitable.

Question 12

"Would you elaborate on the significance of Hegel's synthetic principle, Kierkegaard's experiential principle, Logical Positivism's verifiability principle, Wittgenstein's usage principle, and Popper's falsifiability principle?"

Answer: By Hegel's synthetic principle I mean his attempt to construct a comprehensive metaphysical system that brought together in one grand vision an extremely wide range of diverse elements that spanned the totality of the natural and supernatural. It unequivocally vetoed propositional revelation from a transcendent-immanent God, and in its systematic comprehensiveness it subordinated every concept of God to speculative, philosophical categories. For Hegel "God" was the Absolute which was necessarily subject to the overarching principle of the dialectic. In similar manner, other philosophers have posited a deity on the basis of metaphysical assumptions—invariably, however, at the price of demoting deity to secondary status (e.g., Alfred North Whitehead's subordination of God to "process").

Sören Kierkegaard vehemently opposed the theoretical pretensions of Hegelianism and insisted on the primacy of the individual, personal, and subjective. Not speculative proofs but passionate, inward commitment alone—a "leap" of faith—can avail to put man in touch with the eternal. This commitment is based on a criterionless choice of that which is objectively uncertain. It is not data, or facts, or evidence, or arguments, but an experience of passionate believing in the face of the greatest risk that brings man to the truth—which is not a doctrine but a mode of being, a way of life. Unfortunately, Kierkegaard gloried in paradox (if not in downright inconsistency) and he was never able to show how truth could be distinguished from error, or God-glorifying worship from idolatry.

Logical Positivism's verifiability principle was the claim that the truth of a statement is its method of verification. If a statement was not a tautology or verifiable by sense experience, it was considered meaningless. However, the principle not only made gratuitous assumptions about reality and knowledge but it also nullified itself. Nevertheless, some philosophers, and especially theologians, have sought to justify their claims by complying with the arbitrary demands of the verifiability principle. Since it is inescapably self-defeating, it can pose no serious challenge to Christian theology. But it does continue to exert considerable influence on philosophical unsophisticates who are constantly exposed to the fatuous pretensions of scientism.

Wittgenstein's usage principle is important because it expedited the movement away from Logical Positivism to a preoccupation with language in its multifarious functions. Instead of facile acquiescence to a priori theories about the nature of language, Wittgenstein urged philosophers to examine a given use of a word or sentence. Although language analysis is a vital part of philosophy today, it has not infrequently been vitiated by a specious denial of its own metaphysical presuppositions and implications. Moreover, it has proven to be sterile in resolving the fundamental problems of philosophy, especially in ontology and epistemology. Mapping the use of words and demarcating "language games" (the special and distinctive ways in which words and actions are conjoined) are relatively meager contributions to the crucial issues of truth and knowledge, especially as these relate to theological claims and conflicts.

Karl Popper's falsifiability principle pertains to credibility rather than to meaning. He insisted on the specification of conditions that would serve to falsify a claim. But he did not maintain that if a claim is devoid of such specification, it should be considered meaningless. Rather, he asserted, if conditions of falsifiability cannot be specified, the claim in question cannot be "scientific." The upshot of this, however, is that if purportedly informative claims thereby lack scientific status, they are hardly to be accepted. For even the most credible scientific propositions are merely opinions—provisionally corroborated opinions, perhaps, but opinions nonetheless. No matter how well corroborated a scientific hypothesis may be, it is still refutable—and that refutation is refutable, *ad infinitum*. Hence, knowledge is unattainable. And if scientific propositions are scarcely salvaged from unbelievability, what chance do theological claims have? One might say that they, too, are opinions. But they are not rationally held opinions, for they do not meet (or, at least, do not seem to meet) the indispensable condition of falsifiability which characterizes all opinions which constitute the domain of science. If one is to refute a fideistic interpretation of Christianity, he must expose the untenability of Popper's falsificationism no less than Logical Positivism's verificationism.

Question 13
"You say that philosophy may show that revelation is possible. How can it? Also, would you give an example of how philosophy can undergird certain nonrevelational truth-claims that comport with Christian affirmations?"

Answer: Two main types of arguments have been employed to deny the possibility of divine revelation. First, various attempts have been made to show that God does not, or cannot, exist. This obviously entails the impossibility of divine revelation in the biblical sense. Second, some philosophers have affirmed that God does, or may, exist, but that it is impossible for him to communicate with us, particularly by way of incarnation and inscripturation.

Philosophical assessment of antitheistic arguments since the time of ontological naturalism in ancient Greece has disclosed the gratuitousness of this metaphysical position. In recent years, Jean-Paul Sartre and J. N. Findlay, among others, have vigorously argued for the thesis that God cannot exist. Not one of these antitheistic arguments has survived philosophical scrutiny, however.

The same can be said of the second category, consisting of those views that are both theistic—or at least agnostic rather than atheistic—and that oppose revelation. Assumptions about the nature of reality or knowledge, which underlie such opposition, have been shown to be unwarranted. Deistic or quasideistic perspectives are the most patent examples of this position. Herbert of Cherbury, Thomas Hobbes, John Toland, Matthew Tindal, and Immanuel Kant are some of the better known representatives of this view. However, a considerable number of liberal and "neo-orthodox" theologians—often theorizing in accordance with Kantian prejudices—espouse an antiincarnational or anti-inscripturational revelation from God.

Rigorous analyses of concepts and presuppositions, coupled with thoroughgoing criticism of inferences and extrapolations, have disclosed the fallaciousness of antirevelational arguments. This is the work of philosophy, whether it is done by philosophers or theologians. Positively, philosophical reflection supports the *possibility* of divine revelation, for it discloses the absence of logical obstructions that would preclude it. The only acceptable attitude that is consonant with the possibility of divine revelation is investigative openness to the claim and rigorous examination of the credentials that may accompany it.

One of the most patent examples of philosophy's support of nonrevelational truth-claims consonant with Christian affirmations is the criteriological givenness of the principle of noncontradiction. All Scriptural assertions, including those about God ("God is love," "God cannot lie," "God cannot deny himself," and the like), are uninformative unless the principle of noncontradiction holds objectively and absolutely. The latter is clearly a premise of Scripture, and thus philosophical elucidation and advocacy of it comports with its biblical indispensability.

A theory of irrationalism (a denial of the principle of noncontradiction) is not only incompatible with Scripture but is also self-nullifying, as philosophical analysis reveals. Logicians recognize that if contradiction is allowed, any proposition can be inferred; the affirmation *and* denial of every proposition—even the principle of noncontradiction itself—becomes possible. Hence, no absurdity can be more fundamental than the denial of the principle of noncontradiction.

Question 14

"Why has the pragmatic principle of workability become the chief arbiter of truth and value in the West? And since it is, shouldn't Christian apologists make use of it in defending the Christian faith in a way that is both relevant and cogent in Western culture?"

Answer: Although pragmatism as a philosophical movement has been dead for some time, its influence persists to this day. That influence is probably most evident in North America—undoubtedly because pragmatism's formative thinkers have been Americans, namely, Charles Peirce, William James, and John Dewey. Other historical factors have made their contribution as well. The "work ethic" of Protestantism, coupled with the practical exigencies faced by America's early settlers, must be taken into consideration. No less important is the industrialization and technological advances that the United States has spearheaded in the world. Although the latter are, in part, the result of a pragmatic perspective, a society characterized by free enterprise with its promise of tangible rewards for such accomplishments continually stokes the fires of pragmatism.

Unfortunately, a populace devoid of philosophical insight is easily misled to believe that if a theory works—that is, if it succeeds in bringing about desired results, usually material and measurable—the theory must be true. And from this misinference, it is not difficult to make the extrapolation that *whatever* works is true. This is primarily what the frequently-voiced expression, "that is true for me" means. The "that" is something that *works* for the claimant (it produces good feelings in one, or organizes his thoughts, or enhances his personal relationships, or brings him financial success, or the like). In spite of the fact that philosophical criticism has demolished a pragmatic theory of truth, its followers are legion. Perhaps this should not be too surprising, for a similar situation obtains relative to the scientifically discredited superstition of astrology.

Although a Christian apologist will desire to communicate in a relevant and cogent manner with people in a given society, he will do a disservice to the Christian message if he resorts to an errant notion of truth in presenting it. Indeed, the pragmatic theory of truth is one manifestation of human rebellion against God. It is a way of denying objective, absolute, univocal truth before which man stands responsible and by which he is judged. All three of these modifiers (objective, absolute, univocal) are used here for emphasis, but in reality they are redundant, for they are contained in an accurate definition of truth.

If truth is whatever works for me or for us, then it is man, not God, who determines what is and is not true. The biblical conception of truth is antithetical to the pragmatic notion. If the Christian apologist utilizes false theories of truth, pragmatic or nonpragmatic, he betrays the gospel and jeopardizes the viability of his case.

Why shouldn't a Christian make use of the pragmatic theory of truth? Because it is false and because its utilization is unnecessary. Indeed, the question itself seems to reflect the adverse influence of pragmatism. For it appears to assume that since it is such a persuasive device in our society, the Christian's employment of it will issue in success in converting non-Christians. The Christian should not make use of evil to achieve good, however, nor should he adopt an erroneous theory for the sake of bringing others to Christian truth.

The foregoing can be misunderstood easily if an important caveat is not heeded. The repudiation of pragmatism should not be equated with the denunciation of the "workability" or practicality of the gospel. Legitimate use can be made of the fact that the gospel of Christ is the power of God that results in salvation and changed lives. But this should be done only within the framework of a proper perception of truth and value. The fundamental reason for being a Christian is not because Christianity "works," but because it is *true*. And because it is true, it works with ultimate efficacy—in the sense that it accomplishes all that it promises.

Question 15

"Would you provide an example of a logical incompatibility in a concept of God?"

Answer: Any explicit or tacit predication of a property and its contradictory with reference to the nature or character of God would constitute such an incompatibility. While this is rarely done by theists—and if it is, it is usually done unwittingly—antitheists not infrequently interpret various predications of God as implicitly contradictory. For example, the triune nature of God is often misinterpreted as an affirmation that God is one and three in the same sense. This misconstrual reflects a failure to grasp the ontological distinction between being and person that theologians, however inadequately, seek to indicate—e.g., in the classic trinitarian statement that God is three persons in one Being. The divine attributes of love and wrath have sometimes been interpreted as contradictories. All such allegations should have their surreptitious and gratuitous assumptions exposed as unbiblical. The meaning of such predications can only be provided by revelation, and to the extent that the Scriptures are ignored or reinterpreted from the standpoint of alien philosophical perspectives and categories is it likely that the divine nature or attributes will be misconstrued.

Question 16

"I am not sure exactly why subjectivism, relativism, and reductive naturalism are powerless to oppose Christianity. Would you elaborate on your argument that they are?"

Answer: Certainly their powerlessness does not stem from any lack of rhetorical persuasiveness with which these views have been expressed. Nevertheless, the ability to persuade individuals that a view is true or false frequently lacks correspondence with objective evidence and sound arguments. Persuasion involves many variables, and unfortunately the subjective ones often override the objective ones.

The reason that subjectivism, relativism, and reductive naturalism are powerless to oppose Christianity lies in their intrinsic defectiveness. If one is a subjectivist, he claims that "truth" and "reality" are the products of individual minds. Although there are many versions of subjectivism, they all agree that if there is an extrasubjective reality, it cannot be known. Either the mind is limited to its own contents or in its encounter with an ostensibly external world, it "imposes" its own structures on it so that what it knows is essentially the mind's creation.

In proffering this theory, however, subjectivists implicitly deny it. For they tacitly claim that *this* is reality and that they *know* this *truth* about reality. This state of affairs, therefore, is exempted from being a creation of the mind or merely intrasubjective. And this arbitrary exemption is the self-destructive inconsistency that robs subjectivism of the power to oppose Christianity—or anything else, for that matter. Subjectivism is powerless because it is not a position at all. For any supposed theory that is fundamentally inconsistent can never achieve the status of a genuine position. It is logically unintelligible. Essentially the same critique applies to relativism. It, too, can be shown to be self-canceling.

Reductive naturalism, which has numerous variants, is most easily grasped as the attempt to materialistically explain the whole of reality in terms of physics. It asserts that nothing but space-time or matter-energy exists and that it is manifested in different forms. Either its universe is deterministic or subject to chance.

If reality is deterministic, everything that occurs is the result of physical causes. But if everything is the result of physical causes (which are the only kind of causes, according to this form of naturalism), then the occurrence of a "thought" is such an effect. One is not entitled, therefore, to claim that "naturalism" is true.

The theory itself and believing in the theory are both the wholly predetermined results of physical causes, that is, they are reducible to physical events. Thus there are causes but not reasons for holding that the theory is true. An adherent of such a theory is in no position to argue that the Christian faith is false. Christianity, too, must be the result of antecedent physical causes. Truth and falsity, no less than good and evil, cannot legitimately be predicated of anything. Blind causes warrant neither truth-values nor moral values.

If reality is subject to chance, on the other hand, the possibility of truth-values and moral values is still precluded. Chance is also blind and may be the "cause" of a theory of naturalism and of someone's belief in it. Such caprice means, however, that in the next moment the same person may be "caused" to disbelieve it. Or perhaps in the next moment all theories of naturalism may be totally eclipsed from human consciousness. Hence, a naturalistic theory that is predicated on chance cannot legitimately be claimed to be true. One can only say that he "happens" to believe that naturalism is "true" at this moment. Thus, it is robbed of its power to oppose the Christian faith. Without the admission that there is more than physical causation—dominated by either determinism or chance—one cannot claim that his view is true or that any other view is false. Nor can he appeal to reasons in contradistinction to causes, for his theory precludes the very possibility of such a distinction.

If one is to argue that the Christian faith is false, he can do so coherently only if he acknowledges that there are extrasubjective states of affairs, true and false propositions, sound and unsound arguments, objective knowledge and universal and necessary canons of rationality. But when he does make this acknowledgement, he is confronted with an inescapable question: "Why is reality characterized in this way?" The Christian faith claims to be the only adequate answer—and, indeed, it is. The dismissal of this claim or a refusal to consider the reasons which support it can only be seen as intellectually dishonest and morally reprehensible. Intellectual integrity and moral courage, however, have never been ubiquitous virtues.

2
Crucial Issues

Apologetics and Theology

The fundamental problem of modern philosophy is whether or not it is possible to make a nonarbitrary choice among ultimate starting points. That appears to be a tailor-made incentive for philosophers to interact with theologians. The history of philosophy from Descartes to the present, however, belies any overstatement of such an incentive. The general trend in philosophical inquiry has been away from theological issues to scientific concerns. This is largely because philosophy takes its cue from its cultural milieu, and Western culture is enamored of science—its monumental gains, its vexing problems, and its bittersweet promise for the future.

It is not uncommon for the philosophically naive to unwittingly equate the naturalistic methodology of the sciences with a naturalistic metaphysics. In fact, some philosophers have denied the legitimacy—even the possibility—of metaphysics of any sort. Etienne Gilson debunks such arrogant pontification with an apt metaphor: "Metaphysics buries its own grave-diggers."

Apologetics and, a fortiori, theology have never confronted a more intractable situation in two thousand years of Western history. For both Christian apologetics and theology are avowedly and uncompromisingly metaphysical. Ethical, aesthetic, emotive, sociological, and psychological reinterpretations of the Christian faith are, in reality, covert repudiations. Not infrequently professing an apologetic intention, radical reinterpreters of the Christian faith have actually repudiated it by caricature.

In formulating and applying our apologetics, how are we to insure the avoidance of caricatures of the Christian faith? How should our apologetics be structured and implemented? Are there any biblical norms to guide us in this enterprise? The answer is an unequivocal yes. Scripture provides at least ten cardinal guidelines for apologetics.

(1) The first guideline is the priority of God. This has a twofold reference. In the first place, it refers to God's ontological priority, both in himself as the sole eternal and ultimate reality, and in his relationship to the world as its creator, sustainer, and judge (I Tim. 1:17). In the second place, it refers to God's revelatory priority, both in his universal self-disclosure in the created order and in man's direct awareness of God's reality. Apologetics must not fall into the error of denying this awareness.

Thomas Aquinas denied it and construed the relevant passage in Romans 1 as an inferential proof of the existence of God. He assumed that one could begin without God epistemologically and argue from certain features of the world to the truth of God's existence. This procedure is rare among Protestant scholars today.

Direct awareness of God's reality was denied by Karl Barth primarily on the grounds that the noetic effects of sin obliterated all human capacity for such apprehension. In view of "the infinite qualitative distinction between time and eternity," awareness of God's reality could only be experienced in an act of special, noncognitive revelation. Most evangelicals have rightly rejected this extreme interpretation.

Believing that God is (Heb. 11:6) does not mean that one should postulate the existence of God or that one should live "as if" God exists. Contrary to fideism, it means accepting rather than rejecting what is actually presented to one's nondiscursive awareness of God's objective reality. Such awareness is possible for us—indeed, inescapable for us—because it is inexpungibly resident within the *imago Dei*. Whatever else may have been lost or nullified by the fall of Adam, man's awareness of God (*sensus Deitatus*) has remained. Nevertheless, our response to that awareness has been adversely affected by sin (Rom. 1:18).

If apologetics is to be properly structured and utilized, therefore, it must conform to biblical teaching about God's ontological and revelatory priority.

(2) The second biblical guideline is the significance of the noetic effects of sin. No apologetic perspective can be truly Christian if it underestimates the depth and extent of human depravity. The mind and thinking processes are vitiated by sin no less than the other dimensions of human beings (Rom. 1:18-32; Rom. 8:7; I Cor. 2:14; Eph. 2:3; Col. 1:21). The Bible speaks of a reprobate mind (Rom. 1:28), a corrupt mind (I Tim. 6:5), a blind mind (II Cor. 4:4), and the vanity of the mind (Eph. 4:17).

The depravity of the mind is the source of man's overweening claims to autonomy and self-sufficiency (Jer. 9:23; 17:9). Our Lord crisply states the root motivation of those who reject divine revelation and presume to pontificate about ultimate reality on their own authority: "He who speaks on his own does so to gain honor for himself" (John 7:18). In his sinful estrangement from God, man fancies himself to be God—the quintessence of hubris and the most disastrous satanic seduction of all (Gen. 3:5).

Biblical teaching is unequivocal in its diagnosis of man's most fundamental problem as spiritual and moral (Isa. 59:2; Mark 7:21-23). Consequently, he is an inveterate rationalizer and evader of responsibility. He makes his mind the slave of his motive (John 3:19-21) and wills himself to be supreme—irrespective of truth, evidence, and proof.

In the twentieth century, mankind seems to be carrying "the revolution of the self" to consummate radicalization. There are three prominent facets of that revolution. The first is the assumption that the self is capable of interpreting all of reality. This is most conspicuous in naturalistic philosophy and science. The second is the belief that the self is capable of healing itself of all of its maladies. This is most evident in psychology and technology. The third facet is the presumption that the self is capable of directing itself into authentic fulfillment. This is most apparent in the proliferation of nonbiblical religions and utopian ideologies.

To this worship and service of the creature more than the Creator, Scripture addresses itself with unambiguous directness. To the assumption that the self is autonomously creative, Scripture says that it is "conceited and understands nothing" (I Tim. 6:4). To the pretension that the self is autonomously curative, Scripture says that "he who trusts in his own heart is a fool" (Prov. 28:26, NASB), because "the heart is deceitful above all things and desperately wicked; who can know it?" (Jer. 17:9, KJV). To the presumption that the self is autonomously competent, Scripture says, "it is not in man who walks to direct his steps" (Jer. 10:23, Berkeley).

Man's thinking powers are not only restricted by finitude; they are also in bondage to an incorrigible pattern of sinful self-interest. The greater the relevance of a cognitive object to our relationship with God, the more the natural mind distorts the apprehension of such a reality in order to conform it to the self's controlling bias. Apologetics serves a useful function, but in itself it is powerless to overcome spiritual and moral thralldom (John 8:34, 36; Rom. 8:3).

In connection with the subject of the noetic effects of sin, an important caveat is needed. We must not allow the doctrine of human depravity to eclipse the biblical significance of the *imago Dei*. Merely to concede that there is a residual *imago Dei* in fallen man is inadequate. In a theological or apologetic perspective, the function and limitations of the *imago Dei* must comply with Scriptural teaching. On the one hand, it should not be rendered totally inoperative, and, on the other hand, it should not be invested with exaggerated powers.

Although numerous examples of such an imbalance among apologists can be cited, a not untypical instance is the claim that human knowledge is possible only on the basis of divine revelation. If the referent of the term "divine revelation" is the Bible, two radical deficiencies can be discerned, and they suffice to show the fallaciousness of such a claim. First, since knowledge is not knowledge unless the propositional meaning grasped by it is true, it follows that every propositional meaning held to be true by the unregenerate is actually false. This is patently absurd. Christians and unbelievers do not disagree on every proposition, and when one becomes a Christian, he does not negate *every* proposition that he accepted prior to his conversion.

Second, if one cannot know anything veridically in his unregenerate state, how can he know that the object in which the revelation comes (that is, the Bible as a sensory object) is not a mere intrapsychic image without an independent reality of its own? And if he cannot know whether or not it is an extrasubjective reality, how can he know anything on the basis of it? Thus, without some veridical knowledge, one could not grasp divine revelation. Or to put it differently, if an apprehension of biblical revelation must precede all veridical knowledge, then no one could ever know anything veridically. And this means that he could not even know that veridical knowledge is achievable only on the basis of Scriptural revelation. The claim is self-canceling, therefore, because it can be shown to lead to absurdity.

(3) The third biblical guideline for apologetics is the cognitivity of divine revelation. Whenever the Christian faith has been reduced to mysticism, encounter, or experience, the basis for apologetics has been removed. Neither in the negative sense of defending the Christian faith or in the positive sense of constructing a reasoned case for it can apologetics survive without the recognition of certain truth-claims. Dialectical theologians have tended to deplore apologetics precisely because of their propensity to eliminate propositional content from divine revelation. Not only does the deletion of propositional information undermine the viability of apologetics, however, it also destroys the identity of the Christian faith. The constitutive tenets of the Christian faith are not vague symbols or oblique signs. They are referential meanings that bear the property of truth because they refer veridically to objective states of affairs.

The central concern of every apologist ought to be the justification of the claim that the definitional doctrines of the Christian faith are true. Since nothing is more important than the question of truth, the apologist should not allow his enterprise to sink to the level of sophistry. Nor should he relinquish the task of justification and take refuge in mere proclamation, testimonial, or silence. The latter may be useful as episodic tactics, but they should be employed within the larger context of a full-fledged apologetic perspective. In other words, an occasional tactic must never be substituted for an overall strategy.

Since apologetics is a strategy for nothing less than truth, cognitive, propositional revelation is foundational—not only to apologetics but also to all modes of God's self-disclosure. The apologist prosecutes his calling, then, in the confidence that the Spirit of truth will use the Word of truth to draw and convert men to the One who is the Truth (John 8:32; 14:6; 16:13; 17:17).

(4) The fourth cardinal guideline is the biblical teaching that the Christian's knowledge of God is a matter of certainty, not mere certitude. Certainty is epistemological, whereas certitude is psychological. Certainty is the intellectual apprehension of an objective state of affairs, whereas certitude is a subjective assurance with reference to an object whose ontological status is problematic at best. The apostle Paul stated, "I know whom I have believed" (II Tim. 1:12), not "I postulate whom I have believed."

The experiential basis of the Christian's knowledge of God is twofold. It is constituted both by universal, nonsalvific theistic awareness (Rom. 1:18-21) and by the special givenness of God's reality and saving presence in regeneration and illumination (John 17:3). Faith is essential, not as postulation but as an attitude of sincere and wholehearted trust in the person, work, and word of Christ. This trust is categorially different from postulation. It yields certainty because its object (the one, true God who is revealed in the Lord Jesus Christ) is veridically apprehended by the regenerated believer. God is extrasubjective, transcendent-immanent, eternal, personal Spirit (John 4:24). Knowing that he *is* is logically entailed in knowing him. And knowing him is *knowing* him, not merely believing that he is there. This is to be sharply contrasted with mysticism and other forms of religious subjectivism, for the latter are counterfeits of veridical apprehension of

God—as vivid hallucinations or mirages are counterfeits of veridical apprehensions of actual objects, such as trees, mountains, oases, and so on.

The apostle John says that we "know him who is true," (I John 5:20, NIV), "we can be sure we know him," (2:3), and "we know that he lives in us: We know it by the Spirit he gave us" (3:24). Since this knowledge is not an achievement of ours, but a gift of grace, there is no ground for boasting (Eph. 2:9) and there is no justification for disdain toward those who do not know him. In knowing Christ, we know ourselves and others with a transformed perception (II Cor. 5:16), and nothing is more incongruous with it than a lack of humility and love. Thus, certainty does not entail pride any more than certitude or faith-postulation guarantees humility.

(5) The fifth guideline for apologetics is the biblical balance between God's sovereignty and man's responsibility. The problem is misconstrued if one interprets Calvinism and Arminianism as neat and tidy positions that dispose of theological bafflement in their own self-contained and logically incompatible ways.

In my judgment, the key question in this theological debate is not how one can eliminate the disconcerting paradoxes. Nor is it even whether one can remove them. Rather, the question is: According to Scripture, where should the pivotal *aporia* (i.e., an irresolvable problem) be located? An excessively narrow Calvinism nullifies the significance of the *imago Dei* and founders in its attempt to clarify the meaning of God's justice. An excessively narrow Arminianism lapses into synergism (the union of human effort or will with divine grace) by dissolving the significance of sin's enslavement and by crediting human nature with the power to limit God. It inevitably compromises biblical teaching about God's omnipotence and omniscience.

In striking contrast to both of these extremes, Scripture attenuates neither God's sovereignty nor his justice, neither man's spiritual bondage nor his full responsibility (Eph. 1:11; Rom. 1:20; 9:14-21; 14:12). The problem is not whether God is omnisciently and omnipotently sovereign, just, and loving. No other possibility is exegetically permissible. The problem is not whether man is responsible and guilty. No other alternative is exegetically justifiable. The problem is not whether the two horns of the dilemma are compatible, logically or ontologically. No other possibility is theologically warrantable, for God is not the author of confusion and he can neither lie nor contradict himself (Titus 1:2; II Tim. 2:13). In God there are no incongruities or conflicts. There is, therefore, no *intrinsic* problem.

Nevertheless, there is a problem for us, namely, whether or not we can harmonize the two ostensible polarities. Since the Bible does not harmonize them, we should follow suit and locate the key aporia at the interface of divine sovereignty and human responsibility. This is in contrast to an excessively narrow Calvinism which locates it at the intersection of divine election and divine justice. And it is radically different from a thoroughgoing Arminianism which locates it at the intersection of human depravity and human responsibility. These and other purported harmonizations invariably distort the revelatory truths involved, not because they are inherently irreconcilable but because we do not have all the data that we need to achieve a resolution ("we know in part," I Cor. 13:12) and because we are finite (Rom. 11:33-36). Even if we had the information for which we hanker, we would probably be able to understand it as well as a two-year-old toddler can understand quantum physics.

Not only do some other Christian doctrines have aporetic dimensions, but all non-Christian religions and philosophies (without exception) have their own aporiae—which, unlike those that pertain to the biblical revelation, lack the promise of ultimate resolution.

(6) No apologetic can be truly Christian unless it conforms to Scriptural teaching about the Holy Spirit. *Pure apologetics* is concerned with the objective justification of the Christian faith, irrespective of human response. *Applied apologetics* is the utilization of justificative procedures and data in the actual presentation and defense of the gospel. In contrast to pure apologetics, applied apologetics is marked by a high degree of person-variability. Since the purpose of apologetics only terminates in a ministry to persons, it is radically defective if it fails to accom-

modate itself to the work of the Holy Spirit in convicting and converting human beings.

Scripture is unequivocal in its teaching that apologetics, no less than the proclamation of the gospel, is ineffective without the action of the Holy Spirit upon the human heart (I Cor. 12:3). The Holy Spirit alone can bring genuine conviction of sin (John 16:8-11). He alone can remove the spiritual blindness of man to see the glory of the Son of God (John 16:14; I Cor. 2:14-16; II Cor. 3:17; 4:6). He alone can neutralize the enslaving power of Satan and liberate human beings from the grasp of the evil one (II Cor. 4:4; Eph. 2:2; 6:12; Luke 8:12; Acts 26:18). No apologetic, no matter how well formulated or presented, is a match for the arch-deceiver, for as I John 5:19 states, "the whole world is under the control of the evil one." Not our apologetic systems or skills but only the Spirit of God who indwells us is greater than he who is in the world (I John 4:4).

The communication of the revealed truth of God and the very presence of God to our hearts is the work of the Spirit who produces certainty in the depths of our being (Gal. 4:6; Rom. 8:16). He is not a mere supplement to apologetic adductions or evangelistic preaching. Rather, from the beginning he is the one who uses the proclamation of the Word of God, and his convicting, persuading, illuminating work is a unity.

(7) A corollary of the integral necessity of the Holy Spirit's ministry is the biblical guideline of prayer. If anyone thinks that apologetic arguments can effectively reach men, so-called intellectuals or otherwise, without prayer and the work of the Holy Spirit, he is not only disloyal to Scripture but he also deludes himself. What is indispensable for the apologist and his enterprise is spiritual power (Zech. 4:6; Acts 1:8).

Christ explains much of our failure when he emphasizes the power of believing prayer in combating demonic forces (Mark 9:28, 29). Without him we can do nothing—neither evangelism nor apologetics (John 15:5). The efficacy of our ministry, whatever it may be, waits upon our waiting upon God. The cruciality of prayer is stressed by Christ in connection with our fruitbearing (John 14:12-14; 15:7). Like the apostle Paul, great apologist and evangelist that he was, we should intercede for everyone because God "wants all men to be saved and to come to a knowledge of the truth" (I Tim. 2:1-4). An apologist ought to have a burden like that of Paul's, who said "my heart's desire and prayer to God for the Israelites is that they may be saved" (Rom. 10:1).

(8) The eighth biblical guideline is the primacy of gospel proclamation. Apologetics must not be allowed to supplant the direct, simple, anointed preaching of the gospel, for it, and not intricate argumentation, is "the power of God for the salvation of everyone who believes" (Rom. 1:16). Although all preaching includes some use of logic, and evangelistic proclamation may make substantial use of apologetic elements, apologetics should not be permitted to overwhelm the straightforward, positive declaration of the saving message of Christ, which is succinctly stated in I Corinthians 15:1-4.

Two important reasons serve to justify the priority of nonapologetic preaching. First, since conviction is wrought in the heart of a listener by the Holy Spirit using the Word of God, which is "living and active" and "sharper than any double-edged sword" (Heb. 4:12), the distracting discursiveness of apologetic methodology may preclude the full efficacy of a given instance of preaching or witnessing. And it does this most often by shifting the focal point of concern to something other than the gospel and the individual's need of redemption. We must keep in mind the fact that the vast majority of people believe in God and become Christians without extensive apologetic argumentation.

The second justificative reason for a nonapologetic approach to have precedence is the paradigmatic example of Christ and the apostles. A study of the four Gospel accounts and the Book of Acts is especially illuminating in this connection. In his letters to various churches, the apostle Paul emphatically states his general approach to have been one of Spirit-empowered preaching that centered on Jesus Christ and his redeeming death and resurrection (I Cor. 2:2; Gal. 3:1; I Thess. 1:5; 2:13). The apostle Peter's injunction to engage in apologetics implies that a positive witness is generally given first and that questions are directed to the Christian in response to the nonapologetic expression of his hope in Christ (I Peter 3:15).

Apologetics, then, is ancillary to evangelistic and expository preaching—but that does not mean it is either optional or trivial. Apologetics is a systematic response of the reflective and culturally informed Christian to attacks that inevitably come upon the truth-claims of the Christian faith. In conducting this needed enterprise, the apologist must resist the temptation to translate the Christian faith into an alien frame of reference, whether it is philosophical or religious. A fortiori, preaching must refrain from this subtle distortion of the gospel. As Paul urges, we are to hold fast to the form of sound words—words which the Holy Spirit teaches (II Tim. 1:13; I Cor. 2:13).

Nevertheless, this should not be misunderstood, for one must learn the thought patterns and language of the culture which he addresses. Both relevance and freshness of expression must be valued and cultivated. Maintaining the balance between the moorings of biblical language and the need for cultural relevance is demanding, but the apologist must make that his special concern. This requires intense listening, wide reading, painstaking analysis, deep reflection, persistent questioning, and profound resolve. All of this is essential, however, if the Christian apologist is to adequately defend the faith and refute erroneous theories about God, Scripture, truth, knowledge, nature, man, and salvation (I Tim. 6:20; Titus 1:9).

(9) The ninth biblical touchstone for apologetics is the corroborative role of evidence. The significance and place of evidence in apologetics and evangelism is a highly controverted issue among evangelical thinkers. The first requirement for making an accurate assessment is to notice that Christ and the apostles make use of evidence. Do they do so only to attract and hold the attention of unbelievers? Are evidences of value only to those who already believe? And if the Holy Spirit alone can regenerate, is not an appeal to evidences both superfluous and presumptuous? The broad frame of reference for settling these questions will be dealt with later. At this point, let us seek to discern some of the implications of the Bible's references to evidences.

Of the number of Old Testament instances in which the evidential power of miracles was demonstrated, none is more dramatic than that of Elijah's contest with the prophets of Baal on Mount Carmel. When the people *saw* the fire fall in response to Elijah's prayer, conviction was produced in their hearts and they openly acknowledged that Yahweh is God (I Kings 18).

In Mark 2:1-12, Christ takes the initiative in responding to the skeptical thoughts of some teachers of the Mosaic law by proffering them empirical evidence. The paralytic was healed by Christ for the express purpose that they may "know that the Son of Man has authority on earth to forgive sins" (Mark 2:10). He did not have recourse to fideism or subjectivist reductionism. By this and similar appeals to evidence, Christ has provided a perpetual paradigm for apologetics and preaching. He unequivocally established a relation between empirical data and theological truths. He explicitly states the relevance of evidence—not only for believers but also for unbelievers.

In John 10:25, he says, "The miracles I do in my Father's name speak for me." In John 10:38, he tells his cavilling opponents, "Believe the miracles, that you may learn . . . that the Father is in me, and I in the Father." In John 11:45, we are told that when many of the Jews had seen what Jesus did (specifically, the raising of Lazarus), they "put their faith in him." And in John 12:11, it says that "on account of him [Lazarus], many of the Jews were going over to Jesus and putting their faith in him." Other passages in the Gospel of John that state or illustrate the persuasive value of evidences are 4:53; 5:36; 14:11; and 15:24. John 20:30, 31 explains the purpose for which the miraculous signs were recounted in the book: "that you may believe that Jesus is the Christ, the Son of God, and that by believing you may have life in his name."

The adduction of evidences and logical argumentation does not guarantee persuasion or conversion, however, any more than the preaching of the gospel can insure such results. People may be mere sign-believers without trusting in Christ (John 2:23-25). Nicodemus had not been born again when he went to Jesus with the confidence that God was the author of his miraculous works. But people may also hear the gospel and believe in vain (I Cor.

15:1, 2); that is, their faith may be spurious, since it is not a believing unto salvation (Heb. 10:39; Matt. 13:1-23). Therefore, fideists have no grounds for disparaging empirical evidences and rational justification, since there is no guaranteed response to the preaching of the gospel in contradistinction to the powerlessness of apologetics. This false and unbiblical antithesis is often the result of special pleading. Numerous passages are forced into the procrustean bed of fideism, such as Isaiah 55:8, 9; Colossians 2:8; John 20:29; and I Corinthians 1:18-31. But this can only be done by applying faulty exegesis and truncated theology.

Perhaps the preeminent "proof text" for that point of view is Luke 16:31: "If they do not listen to Moses and the prophets, they will not be convinced even if someone rises from the dead." On the basis that evidence cannot create saving faith, it is inferred that it is superfluous. Now of course evidence is insufficient to bring about anyone's saving conversion, but so is the Bible, or preaching, or giving one's testimony. No one can truly acknowledge Christ as Savior and Lord without the supernatural work of the Holy Spirit in his heart. But let us not confuse necessary and sufficient conditions, and let us not forget that there is a subjective side to conversion.

The point made in Luke 16:31 is that the problem with the rich man and his brothers was not their lack of truth or evidence but their hardness of heart. The mere reading of the Old Testament will not suffice to remove the veil across hard hearts (II Cor. 3:14, 15). Does this mean that the Bible should not be read? Of course not—and no more does it mean that evidences should not be used because they cannot guarantee the removal of adamant opposition. What is needed is a holistic approach to the question of evidences if we are to be faithful to biblical teaching. This means that all of the relevant passages must be contextually scrutinized and harmoniously related.

The role of evidences should neither be minimized nor overestimated. To be sure, our confidence must never be reposed in the inherent virtues of evidences and arguments but in the faithful ministry of the Holy Spirit to use truth to bring men to an awareness of their need and to a conviction of the credibility of the Christian faith. We need to interweave Scripture, particularly the truths of the gospel, into our apologetic witness from the very beginning. Since spiritual needs are met by the Word of God (Matt. 4:4), it must have priority in our ministry to people (Isa. 55:11). This calls for diligent adherence to Paul's prevailing practice: "My message and my preaching were not with wise and persuasive words, but with a demonstration of the Spirit's power, so that your faith might not rest on men's wisdom, but on God's power" (I Cor. 2:4, 5).

Nevertheless, people will continue to raise questions about the reasonableness of the Christian faith. To dismiss these as illegitimate and dishonest is shortsighted. The raising of questions and the pursuit of truth constitute the only alternative to blind faith and self-delusion. Peter's plea in I Peter 3:15 for a reasoned defense of the faith, and Paul's directive in II Timothy 2:24-26 for the Lord's servant to gently instruct others so that they will be led to a knowledge of the truth, should be put alongside Luke 16:31 and I Corinthians 2:4, 5. That is dictated by a holistic approach to the meaning and value of evidences in the Scriptures.

We must be witnesses, for we cannot discursively prove, nor must we coercively persuade. But we must be witnesses of Christ and the truth of the gospel—for which there are intrinsically cogent and objective reasons.

(10) The tenth cardinal guideline for apologetics is the unity of truth. By "the unity of truth" I mean that all true propositions are mutually consistent and that there can be no disjunction of truth into hermetically sealed compartments. All so-called "double-truth" theories are biblically and logically untenable. Nothing can be true theologically that is false scientifically, and vice versa. Nor can anything be true for you that is false for me—unless we are using such terminology as a circumlocution for "you believe something that I do not believe." But believing or disbelieving has nothing to do with truth *per se*. Truth is a property of propositions, not of persons. Propositions are meanings that may be true or false but cannot be both. If they correctly refer to a given state of affairs, they are true; and if they do not, they are false.

The Bible places the highest premium on truth. In contrast to many of the world's religions, which take refuge in mystical ineffability, the Christian faith uncompromisingly rests its case on cognitively knowable truth. We worship the God of truth (Deut. 32:4) whose truth endures to all generations (Ps. 100:5). He has incarnated himself in Jesus Christ who is full of grace and truth (John 14:6). God's Word is truth (John 17:17), for it is given and preserved by the Spirit of truth (John 15:26). Man's basic problem is that he has changed the truth of God into a lie (Rom. 1:25) because he does not love the truth (II Thess. 2:10).

Since the Creator is the God of truth, all truth belongs to him and constitutes a unity. If the meaning of a statement in Scripture is ascertained, it cannot be contradicted by a true extrabiblical statement. The clarity and self-consistency of God's revelation are theological verities of the highest importance. But they are not suspended in isolation from all other truths. One God and one created order mean one truth. And since truth is a unity, no true proposition that is relevant to theological claims should be ignored. For if it is relevant, it may serve a vital evidential function with reference to the Christian faith.

We cannot do anything against the truth (II Cor. 13:8); we can only do something against ourselves if we reject the truth (II Thess. 2:10-13). Armed with the awareness of the indestructibility of truth and with the knowledge that saving truth is found only in the gospel of Christ (Gal. 1:6-9; 2:5), we are to go forth and speak that truth in love (Eph. 4:15).

Questions and Answers

"What is meant by 'the naturalistic methodology of the sciences,' and how does it differ from a naturalistic metaphysics?"

Answer: Whether we speak of the physical sciences or the behavioral sciences, we refer to domains of human inquiry that employ methods designed to answer their questions in terms of immanent factors in the world. A basic operational assumption is that finite events have finite causes, physical events have physical causes, and psychological events have psychological or physical causes. Methodologically, scientists do not seek for supernatural causes, nor do they ask if an event was effected by divine intervention. They look for explanations that bear the marks of immanency, observability, testability, and repeatability. Scientific methodology is unequivocally naturalistic.

The built-in bias of empirical and natural sciences not only favors nonsupernaturalistic explanations, but is incapable of ap-

69

prehending transcendent causes. This is how it should be, however, for the supernatural—in particular, God—is not subsumable under the kinds of statistical regularities which the sciences pursue. The transcendent-immanent God revealed in Scripture cannot be captured in the nets of human inquiry like the planetary orbit of Mars. The biblical God is radically different from pagan deities that are manipulated by magic and sacrifice.

In the scientific quest for control of our environment, it is understandable and legitimate for such disciplines to function according to a naturalistic methodology. In fact, this methodological restriction is indicative of an intellectual modesty that every Christian should seek to foster and preserve. Nevertheless, some scientists arrogantly exploit the legitimate methodological naturalism of their disciplines and wittingly or unwittingly transmute it into an illegitimate ontological naturalism. That is, they assert that there is no reality beyond the space-time world, no supernatural, no God—and they seek to buttress their naturalistic faith by appealing to the successes of scientific methodology. They presuppose that such a method is competent to judge the question of ultimate ontology. Science enthroned becomes scientism, a naive credulousness toward the capacity of scientists and technology to resolve all human problems.

Philosophically and scientifically unsophisticated people—perhaps more than scientists—tend to confuse a heuristic method with a theory about the nature of reality. Since scientists formulate naturalistic "explanations" on the basis of a method that seems to allow for no alternative, the untutored easily fall victim to the erroneous assumption that such "explanations" are exhaustive and irrefutable—when, in fact, they may be neither. In any case, such assumptions betray a gross misunderstanding of the nature of science and epistemology.

A categorial and logical gap separates methodological naturalism and metaphysical naturalism. A decision to investigate the world in a naturalistic way does not entail that the world is naturalistic. A method is a specific way of attempting to reach a particular objective. It can never dictate the nature of reality. Indeed, by its circumscriptions, it is likely to miss some dimensions of reality. There are important questions that lie outside the methodological scope of the physical and behavioral sciences. Too often this has been forgotten, and ostensibly in the name of a given "science," a gratuitous philosophical interpretation of the nature of reality, in whole or in part, has been promulgated. One of the marks of a first-rate education is the impartation of this awareness and the enhancement of the ability to discern the distinction, both as a generic abstraction and in particular instances.

Question 2
"What is meant by saying that Christian apologetics and theology are uncompromisingly metaphysical?"

Answer: Some philosophers make a distinction between ontology and metaphysics, whereas others use the terms synonymously. The former usually employ the term *ontology* to refer to a description of the types of entities that present themselves to human consciousness. Whether these constitute "reality in itself" or whether there is or is not some reality beyond them is considered to be problematic. *Metaphysics* is a term that is used to refer to claims about the existence and nature of "reality in itself"— that is, ultimate reality beyond the restrictions of the phenomenal, space-time world.

Whether the terms are distinguished or are used synonymously, the Christian faith is metaphysical. To anyone who reads the Bible, it is obvious that assertions are made not only about the world of space and time but also about that which transcends it. Every assertion about God is metaphysical. Statements about the ultimate origin and destiny of man—both of which are related to reality beyond the present world—are metaphysical. Statements about the deity of Christ and about the redeeming purpose of his death and resurrection entail metaphysical claims. That is why the denial of metaphysics implies the rejection of the Christian faith.

It should be emphasized that the denial of speculative metaphysics is not being called into question here. Speculative metaphysics is the attempt to establish claims about ultimate reality (such as the existence of God, the "immortality" of the soul, and so on) by means of unaided reason. The Christian faith is not dependent upon speculative metaphysics—which has been variously regarded by Christians with indifference, acceptance, or hostility. Certainly the Bible is devoid of any purely rational attempt to establish the existence of God by, for example, cosmological, ontological, or teleological arguments, as they have come to be known in the history of philosophy. Although the Bible's metaphysical affirmations derive from revelation, they are metaphysical nonetheless.

In the inclusivistic sense of metaphysics (in that it embraces any and all beliefs about the nature of reality or about man and his place in the scheme of things), not only Christians but literally everyone holds views that are metaphysical. Such views may be poorly thought out or they may be well-formulated, they may be tacit or explicit, piecemeal or comprehensive. But no human being capable of reflective thinking is devoid of them. Hence, the important question for every individual is not whether he will hold metaphysical views, but whether the metaphysical views he holds are true. Some of the most vehemently antimetaphysical philosophies (for example, Logical Positivism and some types of Linguistic Analysis) have been shown to be metaphysical in spite of their protestations to the contrary. In fact, no philosophy or religion has escaped metaphysical presuppositions and implications. It is not a liability, therefore, for the Christian faith to be metaphysical. Indeed, as such, it meets the deepest needs of man. The vital question pertains to the meaning and credibility of the Christian faith's truth-claims about the nature of reality, and specifically about man's relationship to God.

Question 3
"Would you give an example of a radical reinterpretation of the Christian faith that actually results in its repudiation?"

Answer: Virtually every heresy in the two thousand years of the Christian era exemplifies this. Friedrich Schleiermacher

(1768-1834) thought that he was defending the Christian faith, but his interpretation of it in terms of "a feeling of absolute dependence" negated the biblical, orthodox meaning of Christianity. He not only failed to defend it but actually renounced it by substituting his own speculative construction for it. This was true of Hegel, whose philosophical system purported to be a sophisticated, if somewhat qualified, defense of Christianity.

In more recent times, egregious examples can be found in R. B. Braithwaite's ethico-linguistic reduction of the Christian faith, Paul Tillich's assimilation of it to monistic mysticism, and in a large diversity of twentieth century theologians, such as Harvey Cox, Thomas Altizer, William Hamilton, Gabriel Vahanian, Paul van Buren, Jürgen Moltmann, et al. Whether the intention is to defend the Christian faith before "modern man" or to deviate from it, a denial of its constitutive doctrines incurs the Scriptural censure of II John 7, 9 (NASB):

> For many deceivers have gone out into the world, those who do not acknowledge Jesus Christ as coming in the flesh. This is the deceiver and the antichrist.
>
> Any one who goes too far and does not abide in the teaching of Christ, does not have God; the one who abides in the teaching, he has both the Father and the Son.

Question 4
"Would you amplify your distinction between the ontological and revelatory priority of God?"

Answer: To say that God is ontologically prior is to affirm that everything but God himself is a derivative being and is dependent for its existence upon him. In his being, God is absolute and ultimate. He is absolute because he is eternal and uncaused. He does not emanate from something more primordial, like "nonbeing," nor does he have any rivals or entities that are coeternal with him. He is ultimate because there is no one and nothing beyond him, superior to him, or externally limiting to him.

He is immutable in his nature and sovereign in his control of all things. From all eternity he is triune in his being.

The affirmation of God's revelatory priority asserts that the reality of God (but not his triunity) is apprehended before any discursive reflection about his existence or nature occurs. It also means that God takes the initiative in revealing himself. In the totality of objects of which human beings are aware, the givenness of God's reality is the supreme apprehension. Human responsibility is predicated on this knowledge, which is not personal fellowship with God but the cognition of his reality as the Creator who alone should be worshiped and to whom each of us is responsible (Rom. 1:18-32).

Question 5
"If man wills himself to be supreme irrespective of truth, evidence, and proof, what is the value of apologetics?"

Answer: To be sure, apologetics cannot accomplish the supernatural work of the Holy Spirit. But the Holy Spirit uses truth, evidence, and proof to communicate the Christian message so that it can be understood (Matt. 13:23) and believed (Rom. 1:16). Without the Holy Spirit, no amount of preaching, witnessing, or adducing of evidence can avail to replace man's exaltation of himself with repentance toward God and faith in the Lord Jesus Christ (I Cor. 12:3). Although the apostle Paul states emphatically that his message and preaching were in the power of the Spirit so that the faith of his listeners should not rest on the wisdom of men but on the power of God (I Cor. 2:4, 5), we frequently read about him persuading and arguing for the cause of the gospel (Acts 9:22; 17:2, 3, 22-34; 19:8; 28:23). No incongruity is involved, however, for he was acting in accordance with the apologetic mandate which he himself enunciated in II Timothy 2:24-26. Truth, evidence, and proof are not inherently efficacious in producing saving faith, but they are instrumentally effective in the hands of the Holy Spirit. Consequently, apologetics should not be underestimated. Of course, it should never be allowed to supplant the proclamation of the gospel, but it performs an essential ancillary function nonetheless.

Question 6
"Would you elaborate on your assertion that no one can know anything veridically if an apprehension of biblical revelation must precede all veridical knowledge?"

Answer: The point of it is to show the self-defeating nature of apologetic positions that claim that their starting point is the Bible. Neither the Bible as a sensory object nor the logical and semantic principles required to identify and understand the Bible can be derived from the meaning of the statements of the Bible— for all of these must be grasped prior to the apprehension of the meaning of any statements of the Bible.

If a given copy of the Bible is the object of my consciousness, I must view it either as an extrasubjective entity or as intrasubjective—or suspend my judgment. In the case of either one of the latter two alternatives, I am not entitled to use an intrasubjective or problematic Bible as a source for deriving objective truths about the nature of reality. If I suppress the extrasubjective givenness of the copy of the Bible as it is presented to my reflective consciousness, I not only make it impossible to justify the use of the Bible as a source of knowledge, I also preclude the possibility of any knowledge of extrasubjective objects. Therefore, if my allegedly absolute starting point is the Bible's statements, which alone can justify belief in an extrasubjective world and in the objectivity of logical principles, such justification can never actually be forthcoming. For if the apprehension of an extrasubjective world and the objectivity of logical principles is not veridical, I can never apprehend the Bible as an object. And, therefore, the Bible cannot be used as the source of claims about reality, including those that assert the existence of an extrasubjective world and the objectivity of logical principles.

If anyone claims, then, that the Bible is the sole and exclusive starting point for all knowledge, he must already have knowledge of the Bible as an extrasubjective object and he must grasp the meaning of at least some of its statements in order to use it as a source for knowledge about reality.

Contrary to what one might expect, this state of affairs in no way serves to diminish the authority of Scripture. In fact, it enhances it. If the Bible is true in all of its teachings—and it is—and if it teaches epistemological objectivism—and it does—then the Bible itself ought to be graspable as an extrasubjective, sensory object before its semantic content is understood. And its semantic content must be understood before affirmations about the nature of reality can be derived from it. In other words, the Bible itself teaches that one *cannot* begin with the Bible as an absolute starting point for all knowledge. Some knowledge must be attainable prior to the apprehension of the knowledge derived from the teaching of the Bible.

The Bible provides revealed knowledge that could not be attained by any other means. In this way, we are able to preserve a high view of the nature and authority of Scripture. For if the Bible taught that it is the absolute starting point for all knowledge, the Bible would be making an incoherent and necessarily false claim. For, as we have seen, that perspective on knowledge is nullified by a fundamental inconsistency. But the Bible teaches a self-consistent and correct view of the nature of knowledge. No epistemological criticism of the Bible can stand, although such criticism of some of its defenders may be entirely justified.

While the Bible is often underestimated and considered to be less than what it claims to be, it is occasionally overestimated and considered to be more than what it claims to be. The Bible is, in the original manuscripts, the inerrant Word of God. But the Bible is not an object to be worshiped. Nor does it claim, in any of its statements, to be the absolute, sole, and exclusive starting point for *all* knowledge. Human beings know all sorts of things before they encounter the Bible, and when someone in the civilized world sees a Bible, he knows that he is looking at a book. And this cannot, in the nature of the case, be derived from or justified by reading statements in the Bible that say or imply the genuineness of such knowledge. The genuineness of such knowledge must be realized beforehand or it cannot be realized at all.

This is what the Bible itself teaches about the nature of knowledge, and, therefore, the findings of the foregoing analysis comport with it. To assign the Bible an epistemological role that it does not claim for itself is to do a disservice to its nature and authority.

Question 7
"Would you clarify your statement that the constitutive tenets of the Christian faith are referential meanings?"

Answer: The constitutive tenets of any position are referential meanings, for they are propositions. A proposition is an assertion that some state of affairs does or does not obtain. A state of affairs is anything that is or is not, anything that does or does not have a certain property, or anything that is or is not related to something in a particular way. Every proposition—which is essentially the meaning expressible by a declarative sentence—refers to a state of affairs. That is why constitutive tenets are referential meanings.

They are *constitutive* tenets because they are the fundamental and indispensable propositions that collectively serve to define a position. If one denies one or more of these propositions, he rejects the position that they constitute. Of course, denial does not entail falsity of the proposition denied any more than affirmation entails the truth of the proposition affirmed. The truth-value (truth or falsity) of a proposition is determined by the state of affairs to which it refers—not by anyone's acceptance or rejection of a proposition, or by belief or disbelief in what a proposition asserts. Every religion and every philosophy has its constitutive tenets. Those of one position may contradict those of another position. In such a case, it is patent that both cannot be true.

The Christian faith is defined by its constitutive tenets, then—one of which is the proposition that there is only one true God. This proposition refers to a state of affairs; it asserts that reality is not exhausted in man or in the world but that there is a Being who is distinct from both. It is the other constitutive tenets of the Christian faith that make it clear, however, that this proposition is not to be interpreted pantheistically or deistically but theistically. Another constitutive tenet is the proposition that the one true God is triune in his being. If these propositions or any of the other constitutive tenets of the Christian faith are denied, one thereby repudiates that faith. If he denies one or more of these tenets but persists in calling himself a Christian or in claiming fidelity to the Bible, he is a doctrinal hypocrite—a heretic.

The chief importance of understanding the constitutive doctrines of the Christian faith to be referential meanings is that they are to be taken as straightforward assertions about the nature of reality. They are not to be interpreted as cryptic symbols or circumlocutions for human imagination or experience. In fact, every reductive reinterpretation (e.g., the attempt to construe all such propositions as indirect ways of stating ethical principles or moral commands or existential decisions) is to be repudiated. Sometimes under the influence of an occult, or philosophical, or antimetaphysical bias, interpreters of the Christian faith will radically misconstrue the meanings of its constitutive tenets. The Christian apologist has the responsibility, therefore, of precisely defining the meanings of these tenets as well as showing the justification for their truthfulness. Biblical exegesis and systematic theology are as vital as logic and epistemology for the apologetic enterprise.

Question 8
"In view of the revelation of God in the incarnate Son, would you clarify your statement that propositional revelation is foundational to all other modes of God's self-disclosure?"

Answer: There is no question about the ontological incomparability of the incarnation of the Son of God. It is unique. There is nothing in any religion that rivals it. The Hindu doctrine of avatars is frequently claimed to refer to the same kind of phenomenon. But anyone who acquires a thorough understanding of the two doctrines in question finds them to be profoundly and incorrigibly different.

Divine revelation by incarnation must be distinguished from

divine revelation by inscripturation. To be sure, there is an analogy between them, but ontologically they are fundamentally different. The incarnation is the coming of the person of the Son of God into the world by virginal conception and birth. Scripture is the special complex of language and meaning by which God communicates his thoughts and purposes. A person is ontologically different from language and meaning, and a person cannot be reduced to words or propositions. The person of the Son of God is unquestionably the supreme revelation of God to man in human history (John 14:9). In no sense, then, is propositional revelation elevated over the Son of God ontologically.

That propositional revelation is foundational to all other modes of God's self-disclosure is entirely compatible with the ontological supremacy of the incarnate Son of God. It is foundational in the sense that any understanding of the incarnation, the person and work of Christ, and, indeed, of all supernatural events is dependent on the communication and apprehension of propositions that refer to these events and explain their nature and significance. The recognition of the ontological preeminence of divine revelation in the incarnate Son is possible only because of the availability of propositional knowledge. Without propositional revelation given through the prophets and through Christ's words, the early disciples would have had no way to grasp the reality and meaning of divine disclosure in the Son of God. Without propositional communication, we would not know that the incarnation took place, that Jesus is the Son of God, that he died and rose from the dead for the salvation of man, that wholehearted trust in him is required to appropriate that salvation, and so forth. It is in this sense that the claim that any other mode of divine revelation has foundational priority is erroneous.

Even to claim that events, for example, are the foundational mode of revelation is to imply dependency upon propositions. Not only is this claim necessarily propositional in character itself, it also relies on reports about such events. And all such reports express propositional meanings. Revelatory events cannot occur in an interpretive vacuum; nor can they signify divine self-disclosure unless their contextual framework is explicitly propositional. Thus, if propositional revelation is relinquished or subordinated to some other criterion, no nonpropositional entity or event can be justifiably designated as divine self-disclosure.

The primary vehicle of God's special revelation in the world has been his inscripturated Word, that is, the sentences and meanings that constitute the documents of the Bible. God propositionally communicated with man from the beginning (Gen. 3:9-19) and propositionally prepared man for his saving acts in the world (Gen. 3:15; Isa. 7:14; 9:6; 53:1-12). Concomitant with those events, and consequent upon them, he has used propositional revelation to explain them (John 12:48; 17:14, 20; II Tim. 3:15-17). We have access to the revelatory significance of God's action in the world by means of inscripturated propositions. And it is through Scripture that we come to know and believe in the Son of God (John 20:30, 31). We believe in Jesus Christ through the apostles' words (John 17:20). These are the reasons why it is essential to affirm that propositional revelation is foundational to all other modes of God's self-disclosure.

Question 9
"It is one thing to define certainty and certitude as contrastive, but is the distinction real and can it be known (with certainty) that God is apprehensible with certainty?"

Answer: That is an extremely important question, for it penetrates to the heart of the new apologetic methodology that I advocate as an alternative to presuppositionism and verificationism. On one level, it is easy for one to grasp the genuineness of the distinction between certainty and certitude. Whenever it is discovered that subjective assurance with respect to a specific state of affairs has been misplaced, an example is provided of certitude that falls short of certainty. If a state of affairs is not as one believes it to be, then he has only certitude, no matter how intense his conviction. Believing something to be the case is a necessary but not a sufficient condition of certainty. Certainty also requires that that state of affairs actually be the case. If one grasps the distinctions delineated in this paragraph, he implicitly acknowledges that certainty and certitude are categorially different. If one understands that an essential factor—namely, that a given state of affairs must obtain in the case of certainty—prevents them from being the same, then he has certainty in his belief that they are not the same.

On one level, then, we know the reality of the distinction by our own experiences of misplaced certitude—for example, we may have felt absolutely sure that the voice on the telephone was that of a particular friend, but then we found out, after further conversation, that it was someone else. Any case of assurance that later turned out to be misdirected is an example of certitude without certainty. But any case of conviction whose referent state of affairs is as one holds it to be is an example of certainty.

On another level, however, we may call into question the certainty that we acknowledge on the **first** level. Often this results from an overreaction to the pitfalls of naive realism—the view that assumes that however something appears to us is the way that it is in reality. A little contemplation of optical illusions and other "tricks" our senses seem to play on us easily dispels acceptance of naive realism. Analysis of the case against naive realism, however, discloses our dependence upon the distinction between certainty and certitude. In order to recognize that a half-submerged, straight stick is not bent as it appears to be, we must apprehend the stick as it is, namely, as straight. A young child may have certitude with respect to the crookedness of the stick in question, but we have certainty with respect to its straightness—if, indeed, we have examined the stick carefully enough to ascertain that it is straight. Thus, *reflective examination* is the key to avoiding naive realism while at the same time retaining realism with respect to the extrasubjective existence of sensory objects. If any state of affairs is called into question, reflective examination—when it is possible—may serve to remove doubt and show that in a particular case one can have certainty.

At this point, however, someone may object and say that his doubts pertain to a third level. Suppose, he says, that on the first two levels everything is part of a dream or dreamlike state. Even the alleged distinction between certainty and certitude, then, is a figment of one's mind. And reflective examination is itself insufficient, for it may be operating within an illusory domain. How is it possible to be certain that we are certain?

It is this kind of question that has seemed unanswerable to a long line of thinkers, who as a result professed radical skepticism or radical fideism. For them certainty is unattainable—even the certainty that certainty is unattainable. Descartes, for example, was profoundly agitated by the claims of skepticism and fideism. His objective was nothing less than the attainment of certainty and a method by which certainty could be guaranteed. He thought that he had found the indubitable bedrock of epistemology in the inescapability of thinking. For even if one says that he doubts everything, he is aware that he is doubting. Of this he is certain. And since doubting is a species of thinking, he can be certain that if he thinks, he exists. Thus, there are certain data of one's consciousness that are indubitable.

Although Descartes made gratuitous assumptions and unjustified inferences, he put his finger on one type of certainty. He saw clearly that consciousness is characterized by certain operations and data, and that irrespective of their ontological status (that is, whether or not any of the data have an extrasubjective source), the data are apprehended by consciousness with indubitability. If he intended to *infer* the existence of the self from the givenness of thinking—rather than understanding the apprehension of the self as noninferential—his argument, "I think, therefore I am," is unsound. Moreover, he erred in assuming that intrasubjective data (e.g., psychological processes, doubting, inferring, remembering, etc.) are intrinsically more clear and distinct than extrasubjective data (e.g., sensory objects, sounds, colors, odors, etc.). Not only is this an insupportable assumption, it is one that creates enormous problems for epistemology.

By arbitrarily selecting from the data of consciousness only those that could be categorized as intrasubjective, Descartes prejudiced the entire case for a holistic and adequate epistemology. A great variety of objects are presented to my consciousness as extrasubjective, and many of them are as clear and distinct (and some are more so) as any intrasubjective data. His arbitrary selection—and the type of selection he made—created an artificial hiatus between subject and object, internality and externality, epistemology and ontology. Once having made this fateful error, Descartes could never successfully cross the gulf he had posited—not even by an appeal to God as the guarantor of knowledge. In fact, his invocation of God to perform epistemological service was one of the initial steps to irreparably crumble under the onslaught of philosophical criticism. The subsequent history of philosophy unfolds under the intellectual impact of "the Cartesian gap." The majority of philosophers and theologians are still trapped in the meshes of the subjective net unwittingly laid for them by Descartes.

The point of this apparent digression into Cartesianism is to highlight the tenuousness of any objection to certainty on this "third level." When certainty is called into question on this level, it is usually because of unwarranted assumptions like Descartes's. Sometimes, of course, it is due to a misconception of the nature of certainty—if one assumes, for instance, that that which is certain must be exempt from suppression or rejection. Anything can be called into question, even if it is done inconsistently or gratuitously. Any statement can be verbally denied, no matter how patent its truth. For example, the principle of noncontradiction has been verbally denied—although such denial must be made inconsistently. That is, without the necessary truthfulness of the principle, no denial can be made. The certainty with which we apprehend the principle of noncontradiction is corroborated by its actual undeniability. One can verbally, but not actually, deny that which is certainly true and one can verbally, but not actually, affirm that which is certainly false. In neither case is the truth or falsity of the propositions in question affected by such verbal denial or affirmation.

Often it is gratuitous theories that dictate the impossibility of certainty. If, for example, one adopts David Hume's theory of knowledge, it will not be surprising if he denies that he apprehends with certainty the page on which these words were written. But if he adverts to the page itself and reflectively examines it in its givenness, the only way he can verbally deny the certainty of his apprehension is by subordinating the lucidity of what he grasps to the a priori theory that precludes it.

Certainty cannot be denied or called into question unless one is *certain* about some things—for example, that he is denying or doubting certainty, and not something else like certitude or doubt or any other object. Also he must be certain about some other things that seem to call certainty into question, and he must be certain that such things are relevant to the question of certainty. Hence, only by inadequate self-criticism or by dishonesty can certainty be rejected. Consequently, the distinction between certainty and certitude is not the result of arbitrary or stipulated definition. It is an actually undeniable distinction, for it is the prerequisite of every attempt to deny it.

The question under consideration also asks if God can be apprehended with certainty. The Bible teaches that the reality of God is known by every human being as he grows into self-consciousness and awareness of the world (Rom. 1:18-20).

That this is an apprehension that veridically grasps the givenness of God's reality is known in the same way that any other apprehension is known—by reflection. Since it can be called into question—as any apprehension can be—relevant requirements must be met to bring the givenness of God's reality to lucidity. First, one should seek to remove or suspend any theories and attitudes that serve to suppress the apprehension (Rom. 1:18). Second, he should meet the conditions that are requisite for grasping God's reality—specifically, reflection on the whole of existence, including intrasubjective, intersubjective, and extrasubjective realities (Acts 14:17; 17:24-29; Rom. 1:19, 20). Not infrequently the lucidity of the apprehension eludes individuals because of an antecedent refusal to subject oneself to moral claims, including the willingness to do God's will if it becomes known to him (John 7:17).

Third, reflective examination of conflicting and corroborating claims should be made to determine their soundness or unsoundness. If the apprehension of God's reality is veridical, no conflicting claim can be sound—and such claims can be shown to be gratuitous, false, inconsistent, or at least problematic. But if a claim is thus defective, it cannot constitute a genuine challenge to the truth of the apprehension. For example, the presence of evil—especially what is called "unjustified evil"—in the world has been used by some antitheists to argue that a perfectly good and all-powerful God cannot exist. In the nature of the case, however, such arguments cannot succeed, for no finite being, without special revelation, can determine what is or is not justified for an omniscient God to do or allow. Since all things are possible to an infinite, all-powerful God, it is possible that in his wisdom he has sufficient justification for permitting evil in the world. He is under no obligation to tell us what it is.

The apprehension of God's reality can not only be shown to be unimperiled by conflicting claims, it can also be shown to comport with the wide variety of data that are grasped by a correct understanding of the world. This is entailed by the unity of truth—all true propositions must be mutually consistent. Although the reflective examination of conflicting and corroborating claims is not essential for apprehending God's reality with certainty, it is germane to the assuagement of doubt that arises from intellectual attacks on theism. For something that is given to consciousness nondiscursively, the adduction of arguments performs an ancillary and corroborative function. Since certainty requires both subjective assurance and the truth or reality of that which is apprehended, unsettling challenges to such assurance should not be ignored.

Question 10
"What is meant by 'an excessively narrow Calvinism' and 'an excessively narrow Arminianism'? Also, would you elaborate on the significance and location of the key aporia?"

Answer: By "an excessively narrow Calvinism" I mean a theology that goes beyond its classical five-point statement to a view that implies that God is the author of evil and that man is devoid of responsibility for his decisions and actions. The sovereignty of God is defended in a way that makes him the cause of evil, in the sense that evil is according to his directive will. For if God is sovereign, he must be the author of all things; literally everything must be directively willed by him. His sovereignty is also defended by totally nullifying the personal responsibility of human beings. Human will can count for nothing, because if it could, it would infringe upon the sovereignty of the divine will. This contention is often buttressed by the assumption that the fall of man has obliterated a functioning, residual *imago Dei.*

Such an interpretation, however, eclipses the meaning of God's justice. It is one thing to assert that God is just, but what intelligibility does such a claim have in view of the assertions that God directively willed evil and that human beings are totally devoid of personal responsibility? Without some knowledge of God's reality and without some individual responsibility for one's response to that knowledge, human beings are hardly fit candidates for judgment. At least, it is difficult to discern any way that such judgment could be just.

By "an excessively narrow Arminianism" I mean a theology that implies that God is neither omniscient nor omnipotent and that man is not fettered by sin but is capable of contributing to the effectuation of his salvation ("soteriological synergism"). Accordingly, since man's choices unpredictably introduce something new into the world, God can neither know what they will be (for them to be known is for them to be fixed) nor can he be in complete control over them (for they may go contrary to his will and therefore limit his power). Since God must await man's free decision, man has the capacity to provide something out of his own nature that makes salvation possible. Some good remains in him in spite of the fall, and only as that good combines with the grace of God is salvation realized—even if that good is only a person's motive or choice. In fact, man's contribution must be an ongoing one—that is, to consummate ultimate salvation in eternity, one must continue to believe or choose or work to the very end of his life. That is thoroughgoing Arminianism.

According to excessive Calvinism, the key aporia (mystery, conundrum) must be located at the interface of God's election and justice. For if God chooses some to be redeemed and some to be lost, and if this divine choice is antecedent to, and causative of, each human being's response to the gospel, then individual human responsibility is pure fiction. Furthermore, since the Bible teaches that everyone must give an account of himself before God at the judgment, and since many will be lost, any attempt to spell out the divine justice in all of this will hardly succeed. The terms of this theological perspective make it impossible for a person to be anything but what he is predetermined, by divine election, to be. Despite its claims to the contrary, excessive Calvinism demolishes human responsibility.

Excessive Arminianism compromises biblical teaching in the opposite direction. By its extravagant view of human nature's character and capacities, it diminishes divine sovereignty to the level of finitude. Irrespective of its disclaimers, this view attenuates the corruptive consequences of sin in man. Nevertheless, since man is the slave of sin (John 8:34), how is he able to produce anything acceptable to God or even freely choose the gospel of Christ? Hence, the pivotal aporia is located, according to this position, at the interface of man's sinfulness and responsibility.

One must not ask, "Which of the two foregoing theological systems should I adopt?" but rather, "Does the Bible teach something different from both of them?" The Bible does not eliminate or mitigate human responsibility as excessive Calvinism does. Nor does it whittle away divine sovereignty as excessive Arminianism does. Moreover, the Bible does not locate the key aporia where these systems assume it to be. But that aporia must be located somewhere, which is why theologians have persistently grappled with this issue. Rather than taking extremist options in coping with the problem, one should adjust neither the sovereignty of God in favor of human responsibility nor human responsibility in favor of the sovereignty of God. Both of these doctrines should be accepted in their full biblical disclosure. Nevertheless, it should be emphasized that there is no contradiction between the two doctrines of divine sovereignty and human responsibility. Contradiction would be involved only if it could be shown that the same meaning is affirmed and denied. This cannot be shown, however, because both our finitude and lack of revelatory data germane to this problem preclude such an analysis.

There are biblical analogs that exhibit other aporiae. For example, the incarnation of the Son of God defies complete analytic elucidation. But we should avoid the errors of denying either Christ's full deity or his full humanity. The history of Christian theology is marked by a succession of theological aberrations that either compromised his humanity in the interest of his deity or compromised his deity in the interest of his humanity. These aberrant interpretations mislocate the crucial aporia.

Docetism (from the Greek term *dokein*, "to seem") denied his humanity and held that he only appeared to be human. The biblical aporia was shifted by it from the interface of full deity and full humanity to the interface of a transcendent *deity* and a suffering, dying, rising *deity*. Conversely, adoptionism held that Jesus was only a man who became the Son of God at his baptism. This view shifted the biblical aporia to the interface of a finite *man* and a perfect, forgiving, redeeming *man* who is worshiped.

The biblical position involves the affirmation of both his deity and his full humanity, the latter being acquired by means of his incarnation (John 1:1, 14). Only if groundless assumptions are made about deity, humanity, and incarnation is it possible to maintain that logical or ontological contradiction is involved in the biblical doctrine of the incarnate Son of God. The appropriate stance is one of categorical denial of any contradiction, while maintaining that there is an aporia located at the intersection of the deity and humanity of the incarnate Son of God.

This approach to biblical teaching is neither obscurantist nor dialectical (in the Barthian sense of asserting contradictories in order to arrive at an adequate or "true" understanding). It is not obscurantist because it does not deny either logic· or the biblical data in the interest of an a priori theory. It recognizes the absoluteness of the logical (a proposition cannot be both true and not true) and ontological (something cannot both be and not be in the same respect) principles of noncontradiction. It also refuses to suppress or distort interpretively difficult data of Scripture.

The location of key aporiae with respect to various biblical doctrines is of fundamental importance if biblical fidelity and theological integrity are to be maintained. Only if we conform to the biblical paradigm in setting forth the terms of a given doctrine can we truly claim to be loyal to the Scriptures. And only if we acknowledge the limitations of our understanding in any quest to achieve full theological systematicity will we evidence the modesty and integrity that are consonant with "knowing in part" (I Cor. 13:12).

Question 11
"What are some examples of aporiae in non-Christian religions and philosophies, and why are they devoid of the assurance of ultimate resolution?"

Answer: *Aporia* is a Greek word that means "no way out, no exit." I use it in a twofold sense. First, there are penultimate aporiae, that is, problems that are irresolvable in this life alone. Second, there are ultimate aporiae, or problems that are intrinsically irresolvable in this life and in the eternal state. Of course, there are no aporiae of any kind for God. He knows and understands all things, including himself. Hence, there is no mysterious "nonbeing" or "brute given" for God—that is, nothing either opaque to him or coexistent with him as some kind of rival or limiting entity. But by their very nature, finite minds confront aporiae in every direction they turn. And we do not even know where to draw the line between penultimate and ultimate aporiae, in the sense of exhaustively and undubitably classifying every aporia in one category or the other. In fact, this problem is a penultimate aporia itself.

There are some aporiae that we can definitely designate as ultimate. For instance, we will never fully understand the nature of God. Only an infinite mind could understand an infinite being, and in the eternal state we will still be finite, even though our knowledge and capacities will have immeasurably increased. We will not become divine; God will remain the only infinite being.

An example of a penultimate aporia is the problem of individual suffering. Although in this life I may never understand why

I was desperately ill at a particular time and place, I anticipate a disclosure of God's purpose when I enter his presence beyond this life. Scripture indicates that Job did not initially understand God's purpose in allowing him to suffer. But apparently he was later enlightened by special revelation.

Every religious and philosophical perspective has its aporiae. For example, monistic Hinduism posits Brahman—an undifferentiated, impersonal Absolute—as the sole reality. How it is known, how it can be referred to (in view of the fact that it has no attributes but yet it is supposedly not nothing), how it can produce a world of differentiated entities, how the world it produces is "illusory," and so forth—all of these are aporiae.

If one were to take Marxist philosophy as another example, he would find a number of irresolvable problems: how matter can be self-organizing, how it can produce mind, how the dialectical process got started, why it will end when a classless society is achieved, and so on. All such views which deny an omniscient and personal God and repudiate the posthumous persistence of individual consciousness are obviously devoid of the assurance of ultimate resolution. Without an all-knowing God for whom there are no aporiae, there is no one who can resolve them. And without personal survival beyond death, there is no one for whom they can be resolved. But even non-Christian religions and philosophies that affirm an omniscient, personal God and individual survival after death have no assurance that their aporiae will ultimately be resolved. For only in the Christian faith is there sufficient evidence to justify such an expectation. The conquest of sin and death by the risen Christ and a rationally credible Bible provide that assurance. In the person of Christ and his resurrection both the infinite, personal God and the individual's survival of death are demonstrated. Thus, the ground of assurance is not arbitrary philosophical speculation or gratuitous religious claims, but is historically corroborated revelation.

  Question 12
"I found myself incredulous when I heard your statement that 'all preaching includes some use of logic.' Most of

the preaching that I hear is anything but logical. Please comment."

Answer: It is apparent that we are using the word *logic* to mean different things. You seem to restrict it to rational consecution, that is, sound analysis and valid inference. I agree that the absence of logic, in this sense, is sometimes conspicuous in preaching. More lamentable, however, is the arrant violation of logical canons of good reasoning. The Bible speaks approvingly of "the foolishness of preaching," but it never extolls "the preaching of foolishness."

Nevertheless, even foolish preaching—if it has any meaning—involves the use of some logic. For to utter one meaningful word or statement is to exemplify certain logical canons, such as the principles of identity, noncontradiction, and excluded middle. To be illogical, in the sense of asserting contradictories, requires logic on a more fundamental level. That is, unless a statement is meaningful, it cannot be the contradictory of any other statement. But to be meaningful, a statement must conform to certain elementary logical principles.

Question 13
"What does it mean to speak of 'truth's indestructibility'? Doesn't a true proposition, which by definition asserts something about a state of affairs, become false when that state of affairs changes?"

Answer: By its very nature, truth must be unchanging. A proposition is a meaning, not a sensory object (such as a tree, or a sound, or a sentence) and not a psychological state (such as thinking, or remembering, or fearing). Both sensory objects and psychological states change, but meanings are timeless. It is not only truth that is timeless; falsity is timeless, too. Thus, some states of affairs change and some do not. But even when a proposition (a timeless state of affairs) refers to something sensory or psychological (temporal states of affairs), the proposition does not become temporal. Although propositions cannot change, some propositions refer to states of affairs that do change—sensory and psychological states of affairs have, respectively, space-time coordinates and temporal coordinates. Insofar as such coordinates are integral to the state of affairs, a proposition refers to them in referring to the state of affairs.

Propositions do not change, then; they refer either correctly or incorrectly to states of affairs. For example, p is the true proposition that asserts that my nephew is under five feet tall. Ten years from now, he will be over five feet tall. Does this mean that p will become false? By no means. Notice the different coordinates involved. The first proposition refers to my nephew at the present time. The second proposition refers to my nephew ten years in the future. These are two different propositions, not one proposition that changes from truth to falsity. Since propositions may refer to different kinds of states of affairs—that is, those that are spatio-temporal, solely temporal, or nonspatial and nontemporal—it is easy to forget that what may characterize the referent state of affairs does not necessarily characterize the proposition that refers to it. Some states of affairs are destructible (that is, they may change), but all propositions are indestructible. In this sense, we can do nothing against the truth (cf. II Cor. 13:8). Every proposition is true or false irrespective of changing states of affairs and despite our attitudes and actions. What we ought to do, therefore, is make sure that we accept true propositions and reject false ones.

3
Crucial Approaches

Presuppositionism, Verificationism, and Veridicalism

After two thousand years of debate on the relation between faith and reason, Christian apologetics has become polarized into two incompatible approaches. Although representatives of each position would undoubtedly disavow a polemical radicalization of apologetics into a forensic assault on non-Christians, they would not see eye to cye on the epistemological structure of the Christian faith. And that underlying difference would lead them to forge different apologetic strategies.

On the one hand, presuppositionism holds that initial assumptions determine the nature and applicability of all criteria, with the result that one must begin with the basic doctrines of the Christian faith if he is to get to Christianity at all. On the other hand, verificationism contends that there are neutral criteria by which one can establish the credibility of the Christian faith. Presuppositionism emphasizes postulation and coherence, whereas verificationism stresses empirical evidence and inductive justification.

The problem created by the incompatibility of these two

apologetic approaches falls under the rubric *metapologetics*. I employ this neologism to refer to the field of inquiry that examines the methods, concepts, and foundations of apologetic systems and perspectives. The subject matter of metapologetics is apologetics, whereas the concern of apologetics is to commend the Christian faith to non-Christians by exhibiting its intelligibility and credibility, especially in response to objections and criticism directed at its most fundamental premises.

The metapologetic question that asks how the Christian faith should be defended is compounded today by a philosophical perspective, rooted in Popperian epistemology, that condemns as irrational and misconceived the very attempt to justify a position. Fashioned recently by W. W. Bartley III, a follower of Karl Popper, nonjustificationalism contends that all other positions, whether religious or philosophical, involve a retreat to commitment. The very structure of such perspectives is authoritarian because they erroneously believe that certain sources of "knowledge" or certain criteria of truth serve as ultimate authorities in justifying truth-claims and settling disputes. By stopping the justificational regress at any point, says Bartley, one *arbitrarily* commits himself to certain starting points. But there are no starting points that are held universally or that have not been criticized and rejected by some thinker. One cannot vindicate them, because there is no higher court of appeal. Since they are ultimate, they cannot be justified, and their embracement is an irrational and fideistic act. But a position that cannot overcome fideism is unable to refute skepticism.

Bartley contends that the history of intellectual thought has been dominated by a question that begs authoritarian answers, namely, "How can we know such-and-such to be true?" The only alternative to an infinite regress, which can justify nothing, is the stipulation of some authority, intellectual or otherwise. But, according to Bartley, Popper has shown us the way to a more adequate understanding of reason as criticism. The entire enterprise of justification must be scrapped and replaced by an endless process of refutation. There simply are no infallible authorities. There are only hypotheses, none of which is verifiable and all of which are refutable. Since only statements can serve to falsify statements, and since every statement is a theory, every statement is open to falsification. Truth can never be knowingly attained but remains an elusive ideal and a regulative notion. Since whatever is used to refute any given theory is susceptible of future refutation, one need not be committed to anything.

A Christian, like every other non-Popperian, then, is an irrationalist because he is committed to an absolute authority, which, according to Bartley, is specious. Bartley's nonjustificationalism, which he calls "comprehensively critical rationalism," supposedly undermines the justificationist's *tu quoque* argument. That is, no one can say, "I have my starting points but *tu quoque*, 'you also' have your starting points." Bartley maintains that he has no irrefutable starting points, no ultimate touchstone to which he is committed.

Nonjustificationalism is an incoherent position, however, for it must concede the possibility that criticism can refute criticism, logic can refute logic, and refutability can refute refutability. By turning the theory upon itself, it can be shown that it reduces to absurdity.

In order to answer the key metapologetic question, "Can the Christian faith be justified, and if so, how?" a threefold thesis must be established.

(1) The first we have already noted, namely, that the attempt of nonjustificationalism to dispense with irrefutable "commitments" or starting points is a failure, and justification is not only possible but necessary in every promulgation of a truth-claim. That is, whenever a truth-claim is made, the claimant is under a rationality norm to provide justification when it is expected or requested.

(2) It also needs to be shown that every religious and philosophical view, including the most radical skepticism, explicitly or implicitly acknowledges certain *universal givens*, and these givens are points of reference for all rational justification.

(3) Although a particular given can be the object of one's awareness without reflective corroboration of its authenticity, it should be shown that the claim that it is veridically apprehended

cannot be justified without demonstrating how it is congruent with universal givens.

Presuppositionism and verificationism fail to do justice to the epistemological significance of the special givens of the Christian faith and the universal givens of rational experience. To overcome their failure and to achieve a proper biblical synthesis of special and universal givens, I forge a third alternative, which I term *veridicalism*.

First, it is important to be clear about the nature of the apologetic methods known as presuppositionism and verificationism. The term *presupposition* is generally understood to be a basic assumption or starting point that is taken for granted. Presuppositionists maintain that faith is always prior to knowledge. Systems of geometry perspicuously exemplify this relationship: theorems are deduced from axioms and definitions which constitute the fundamental starting points of each system. The axioms are not provable. They are postulations. Similarly, every world view, every philosophical and religious perspective, is based on one or more primordial assumptions.

Verificationism holds that there are neutral criteria which can be invoked to verify or falsify a position. The Christian faith is said to be verifiable, that is, highly probable, with respect to publicly accessible evidence. Great importance is attached to "empirical historiography" and its competence to assert the probability of the resurrection of Christ. By way of contrast, presuppositionism insists that since no one can get outside *every* perspective to make a comprehensive judgment on all positions, the only place for a Christian to begin is with Christian tenets. Since all putative facts must be interpreted from some theoretical standpoint, according to presuppositionism, why shouldn't that standpoint be the Christian faith?

But the verificationist asks why that standpoint *should* be the Christian faith. If there are no neutral criteria, the question cannot be answered, except in terms of obscurantistic fideism. Verificationism and presuppositionism are contradictory positions, then, as their respective affirmation and denial of neutral criteria indicate.

Summarizing the respective merits of these two evangelical apologetic methodologies will enhance our understanding of them and their differences. Eight important strengths are readily discernible in presuppositionism: (1) it perceives the crucial role of presuppositions in creating perspectival systems; (2) it recognizes the pervasiveness of assumptions in interpreting data; (3) it vigorously contends for the absolute ultimacy of the Triune God; (4) it lays heavy stress on the epistemological primacy of God's self-revelation in Scripture; (5) it intransigently opposes man's claim to autonomy; (6) it takes the noetic effects of sin with full seriousness; (7) it seeks to avoid the reduction of man to intellect; (8) it attempts to do full justice to the biblical teaching that the regenerating work of the Holy Spirit is indispensable for one to have saving faith.

Verificationism also has its strengths: (1) it is cognizant of the vital importance of empirical content in any world view; (2) it allows for the possibility of challenging presuppositions by logical and empirical considerations; (3) it seeks to avoid radical skepticism by maintaining the unity of truth; (4) it recognizes the unavoidability of making use of ordinary ways of knowing in order to become aware of God's self-revelation in Scripture; (5) it perceives the epistemological importance of avoiding reductionistic fideism; (6) it takes the *imago Dei*, in its residual structure, with full seriousness; (7) it seeks to provide a basis for communication and dialogue with non-Christians; (8) it emphasizes the culpability of man in exercising his will contrary to the truth that commends itself to reason.

Against this catalog of contrasts, we can understand why presuppositionism generally finds Calvinism more hospitable and verificationism feels more comfortable with Arminianism. These are only tendencies that reflect a gravitational pull in the respective directions, and of course there are some exceptions. In any case, presuppositionism especially feels the magnetic tug of divine sovereignty, whereas verificationism is strongly drawn toward divine justice. Their divergent approaches seem to accommodate and comport with the stellar positions of these respective doctrinal emphases.

A brief statement of the weaknesses of both apologetic perspectives should suffice to indicate why they are unsalvageable.

(1) Presuppositionism can never be pure, for it operates with a principle of adequacy that is logically prior to the apprehension and utilization of biblical statements. Presuppositionists claim that their position alone is *adequate* to epistemological and biblical data. Therefore, the formal principle of adequacy functions as a neutral criterion. Since it is recognized and applied as a universal justificational norm in the epistemology of non-Christians, the presuppositionist's claim that there is no overlapping of knowledge or criteria between the Christian and non-Christian is incorrect.

(2) Presuppositionism suffers from another methodological impurity. The very act of presupposing or postulating requires a nonpostulate. The principle of noncontradiction cannot be postulated, simply because it is a necessary condition of *every* act of presupposition or postulation. It is primordially required for both the semantic intelligibility of the terms of any presupposition and the logical intelligibility of the proposition that constitutes the presupposition. Without the principle of noncontradiction, as a universal and necessary given, it is impossible to formulate a presupposition. And with the inclusion of one nonpresupposition, there can be no pure presuppositionism.

Let us try for a moment to rehabilitate presuppositionism by distinguishing two types. *Comprehensive presuppositionism* claims that all of its starting points are postulational, including the principle of noncontradiction. As we have seen, this is patently absurd. *Limited presuppositionism* recognizes the principle of noncontradiction as an indispensable, universal criterion. Accordingly, the principle is not derived from the Bible but is prior to it as the condition of grasping and explicating its contents. The limited presuppositionist builds his case on the contention that the Christian faith is self-consistent and that all other systems are inconsistent because they violate the principle of noncontradiction.

Nevertheless, limited presuppositionism is untenable. First, because self-consistency alone cannot guarantee the truth of a metaphysical perspective. And second, because even if all other

known metaphysical positions are shown to be logically incoherent, that is not sufficient to establish the truth of one's own
presuppositional system. The first defect follows from the distinction between truth and validity. The second follows from the
argumentum ad ignorantiam fallacy: in an open or unlimited
universe of discourse, the refutation of any number of other systems or theories cannot, by itself, establish the truth of one's own
position. We can know that mutually incompatible systems cannot both be true, but the principle of noncontradiction does not
guarantee that we have all the systems before us. Furthermore,
limited presuppositionism fails because there is no way to preclude the gratuitousness of its basic postulates.

Does verificationism fare any better? To answer that question,
let us distinguish its two types from the outset. *Comprehensive
verificationism* claims demonstrability for its arguments for the
existence of God, and on that basis it seeks to establish the probability of the truth-claims of the Christian faith. *Limited verificationism* maintains that both the existence of God and the truth-
claims of the Christian faith can only be shown to be probable.

Comprehensive verificationism does not succeed because of
the unsoundness of theistic arguments. Beginning with a mere
concept of God, one cannot validly infer the extraconceptual or
actual existence of God. Beginning with a finite world, one cannot
deductively arrive at an infinite God. In spite of the great ingenuity
expended in attempting to frame a sound theistic argument, none
has escaped the charge of smuggling in question-begging assumptions. Although there are recurrent attempts to rehabilitate
the classic theistic arguments (e.g., the cosmological argument
by Norman Geisler and other Thomists, the ontological argument
by Charles Hartshorne, the teleological argument by Richard Tay-
lor), they are rejected by most philosophers. And if one's case for
the probability of the Christian faith rests on an antecedent argument for the existence of God, the attempted justification is
stillborn.

Limited verificationism makes more modest claims, but it is
also vulnerable to nullifying criticisms. It makes no pretence of
achieving intellectual certainty, for by its restriction to induction

it must concede that premises cannot establish a conclusion with logical necessity. Its first defect is that it bases its case on fideism. If the presuppositionist postulates metaphysical assumptions as his starting point, the verificationist postulates epistemological assumptions as his starting point. Verificationists admit that they can only *assume* that there is a rational structure that is universal and correlative with reality. Limited verificationism fails because its basic epistemological assumptions are insusceptible of rational justification, for assumptions cannot be used to justify themselves.

The second major defect is the position's failure to avoid metaphysical assumptions in spite of its disavowal of them in its foundations. Verificationists say that they accept "the scientific method" as the fundamental heuristic technique for discovering truth. But that method operates only on the basis of presuppositions about the nature of empirical data (e.g., that the world is structured), about the relationship between the mind and the world (e.g., that subjective interpretations can be tested by objective data), and about ethical principles, such as the normative claim of honesty over other interests. Such presuppositions are unavoidable, whether one interprets "the scientific method" according to a hypothetico-deductive model or according to an inductive model. The logical and ontological principles of noncontradiction, the law of parsimony, the regularity of nature, causal relations, and ethical norms are essential prerequisites of authentic scientific research. This is a clear indication that metaphysics and epistemology are distinguishable but inseparable. Metaphysical presuppositions are implicit in every epistemology, and epistemological presuppositions are implicit in every metaphysics.

Since limited verificationism professes to arrive at metaphysical conclusions solely on the basis of epistemological premises, careful scrutiny reveals a crisis of identity. If empirical data are susceptible of alternative interpretations according to different metaphysical frameworks, how can one arrive at the Christian faith on these terms without begging the question? Insisting that we must begin without God in our premises, the limited verificationist no less than the comprehensive verificationist can never get to God in the conclusion.

All four types of presuppositionism and verificationism tend to confuse certainty and certitude. With respect to Christian truth-claims, presuppositionism cannot achieve certainty because it is based on postulates, and verificationism cannot attain certainty because it is based on induction. Since presuppositionism cannot remove verificational elements and since verificationism cannot eliminate presuppositional elements, we must ask if there is a way to transcend the stalemate between the two positions.

The first step in breaking the deadlock is to distinguish, as *veridicalism* does, five starting points. When one asks an apologist, "What is your starting point?" he asks an ambiguous question. The following taxonomy of initial points of reference will elucidate the significance of this judgment.

(1) There can be only one *ontological* starting point for the Christian, namely, the Triune God. He alone is eternal and all else was made by him and depends upon him.

(2) The *epistemological* starting point is personal awareness, focused in sensory, introspective, and intellective apprehensions and structured by the *imago Dei*, which, however, is adversely conditioned by sin.

(3) The *justificational* starting point for the Christian faith is the special givenness of God's cognitive revelation within the context of universal givens.

(4) The *interpretive* starting point is the set of Christian credenda which serve as the frame of reference for understanding God and the world he has created.

(5) The *methodological* starting point for the Christian apologist is the chief focus of a culture's (or group's or person's) problem-situation.

The second step in ending the stalemate in question is the recognition of the distinction between givens and assumptions. What is a given? Generically described, it is whatever (1) presents itself to awareness (i.e., is not postulated or based on postulation), and (2) does so directly (i.e., without being inferred or derived from discursive reasoning), and (3) can be veridically corroborated by reflective examination of it and of its comportation with other givens. Stated succinctly, a given is a veridically apprehensible state of affairs.

No position can escape such givenness, not even the most radical skepticism. To deny or doubt that there are givens is to tacitly acknowledge givens. Inextricably embedded in presuppositionism are the givens of logical principles: noncontradiction and coherence. In addition to implicitly acknowledging these givens, verificationism also admits the givens of empirical data. And it needs to be emphasized that if something is a given, it cannot be postulated or asserted as probable.

The third step in forging veridicalism is the application of the distinction between givens and postulates. It is wrongheaded to construe the dictum, "I believe in order to know (or understand)," to mean that I cannot know anything unless I first believe something. On the contrary, I must first know (that is, I must be reflectively aware of) something before I can believe in anything. I cannot have faith in reasoning unless I am first aware of reasoning. I cannot have faith in my senses unless I am first aware of my senses. I cannot have faith in the gospel or in the Bible unless I am first aware of the gospel or the Bible. The precedence of knowledge over faith, in this sense, must not be confused with the priority of faith over understanding in another sense, as indicated in I Corinthians 2:14-16. Also note the sequence in Isaiah 43:10: ". . . that you may know and believe me and understand that I am he."

Since faith, in its fundamental biblical meaning, must have objective content (I Cor. 15:1-4), it cannot be separated from the *reflective awareness* of that content—which is its antecedent condition (Matt. 13:23).

The skeptic and fideist agree in their contention that knowledge and rational justification are unattainable. They differ in that the former says he will suspend his belief concerning all things and the latter says he will believe some things. Both of them hold incoherent positions: the skeptic because he must know something in order to doubt anything, the fideist because he must know something in order to believe anything.

The fourth step toward the formulation of the apologetic method of veridicalism is the analysis of presuppositions into four major categories: (1) self-evidencing givens which are of two types: universal givens (e.g., the principle of noncontradiction, perceptual objects, and so on) and special givens (e.g., biblical revelation, which is self-attesting to believers only); (2) systematic postulates (e.g., the Kantian assumption of noumena), (3) heuristic hypotheses (e.g., conjectures that are subject to empirical tests, as in a hypothetico-deductive scheme); (4) forensic assumptions (e.g., the purely functional appeal to premises for the purpose of testing for validity or for indicating propositional preconditions).

On the basis of the four preceding steps, we are in a position to formulate veridicalism. Having distinguished generally conflated meanings of the term "presupposition," and having seen the inescapable distinction between givens and postulates, we can discern how the justificatory process can escape the alleged infinite regress that leads the skeptic to suspend judgment and the fideist to stop arbitrarily at some point. Refutation and corroboration are possible when universal givens can be brought to bear on particular truth-claims. And when those truth-claims are determinative of a particular perspective, that perspective can be falsified or substantiated.

The main distinguishing feature of veridicalism is *its justificative unification of self-evidence and corroboration.* It differs from presuppositionism in three important respects: (1) it removes the semantic ambiguity of the term *presupposition;* (2) it explicates self-evidence by showing that it is indispensable to all knowledge, Christian and non-Christian; and (3) it includes formal and material corroboration as an *integral* dimension in the justification of the Christian faith.

Veridicalism differs from verificationism in three crucial ways: (1) it begins with the reality of God as a universal given and with the constitutive content of the Christian faith as a special given along with universal epistemological and ontological givens; (2) it rejects that unwarrantable restriction of self-evidence to empirical data; and (3) it dispenses with the allegedly fideistic status

of neutral criteria by showing the relevance of self-attesting givenness to corroboration. Certainty issues from self-evidencing givens, and justification stems from the union of the special givens
of the Christian faith with relevant universal givens—whether
empirical or non-empirical.

Universal awareness of God, which is explicitly taught in the
first chapter of the Epistle to the Romans, is mediated nondiscursively through the created order, which includes man and his
internal life. This awareness is as indefeasible as is self-awareness,
for in similar manner the self's reality is known with *certainty*
although it can never be arrived at inferentially.

Presuppositionism errs in its tendency to interpret rational
justification as the application of human criteria to divine truth,
thereby making it scandalously reprehensible for man to set himself up as judge over God. Verificationism, on the other hand, is
so enamored with discursive justification that it considers any
claim to self-evidence to be a form of fideism—arbitrary and
irrational, in the final analysis. Veridicalism harmonizes the two
principles of self-evidence and discursive justification as comple-
ments in a coherent perspective. Since the Bible teaches that this
is God's world, it is gratuitous for presuppositionists to charge
that a corroborative appeal to universal givens or extrabiblical
criteria and data accords autonomy to man. If man is aware of
something, it does not follow that he created it or that it is the
product of his sinful nature.

In the mere explication of the Christian message there is an
unavoidable appeal to semantic and logical intelligibility, truth-
values, historical data, and relevance to human needs. These are
corroborative points of reference that are not created in the act
of preaching or in the impact of the gospel on a listener. They are
universally given objectivities that the Holy Spirit uses along with
the special given of the gospel's content in persuading human
beings to place their faith in Christ. Since there are extrabiblical
truths, and since truth is formally one, veridicalism holds that it
is legitimate to appeal to corroborative factors which are available
to man universally.

Veridicalism makes an important distinction between neutral ground and common ground. Neutral ground consists of the entire category of universal givens. Any attempt to construct an accurate natural theology proves abortive, however, because of man's sinfulness and hostility to God (Rom. 1:28). Every regenerate Christian has been liberated from the suppression of the truth about God, but every unregenerate person is in bondage to that suppression. This means that there is no neutral person—no individual who is neither accepting nor rejecting the truth about God that is universally given to human consciousness.

As there is a categorial difference between proof and persuasion, logic and psychology, certainty and certitude, so there is a fundamental distinction between neutral and common ground. There is neutral ground ontologically (i.e., there are actual states of affairs) and epistemologically (i.e., there are true propositions and objective logical principles), but not spiritually. By way of contrast, common ground is anything in human experience that can be legitimately made a fulcrum for showing the relevance of the gospel, ranging from personal needs to cultural patterns of thinking and acting. As the Holy Spirit uses the truth as neutral ground, so he uses the area of personal need (such as a sense of guilt, loneliness, ill health, a brush with death, or the like) as common ground in the process of convicting and persuading a person who is not neutral and who holds some presuppositions that are incompatible with the Christian faith.

It is true to say, "Either God or man is ultimate in any system," but if such a statement is interpreted in an unbiblical way, it can lead to gross error. While veridicalism emphasizes the ontological discontinuity between the Creator and the creature, it resists the extreme antithesis between God and man that virtually denies the residual *imago Dei*, actually denies any univocity of knowledge common to God and man, and inevitably denies the unity of truth and being in the nature of God. Nevertheless, veridicalism adamantly refuses to negotiate the absolute autonomy of God.

No more fitting reminder for all who reflect on apologetics and theology can be found than Romans 11:33-36:

Oh, the depth of the riches, the wisdom and
the knowledge of God!
How unsearchable his judgments,
and his paths beyond tracing out!
"Who has known the mind of the Lord?
Or who has been his counselor?"
"Who has ever given to God,
that God should repay him?"
For from him and through him and to him
are all things.
To him be the glory forever! Amen.

Questions and Answers

Question 1
"Exactly what do you mean by a polemical radicalization
of apologetics into a forensic assault on non-Christians?"

Answer: The nature and function of apologetics have
been variously conceived by Christian thinkers in the last two
thousand years. Some of them have understood it as a sustained
intellectual attack on the tenets of contemporary rivals. Merely to
expose the fallacious assumptions and erroneous conclusions of
the positions of others is necessary but insufficient as the apologetic task. Even with the further role of responding to critical
questions about the Christian faith, apologetics is inadequately
characterized. If one conceives of the task of apologetics as either
one or both of these functions, he thereby reduces the discipline
to a polemical assault on non-Christians and their views. This is
what I mean by the expression in question.

In the broad sense, apologetics encompasses epistemology and
ontology. The apologetic task is not fulfilled if the positive role of

systematically constructing an epistemology and an ontology is neglected. Explicating the nature of knowledge and describing structures of reality are not peripheral but essential apologetic responsibilities. They should be developed systematically—not in piecemeal fashion—and they should be explicated prior to the specific intellectual engagements of the Christian with the non-Christian. To omit this dimension of apologetic inquiry is to radicalize or reduce its role to a function that cannot stand alone intellectually. In the give-and-take of debate in the pursuit of truth, reflection ineluctably drives inquiry to the deepest levels of epistemology and ontology. Unfortunately, evangelical apologists have been relatively weak in these areas.

Question 2
"What do you mean by 'the epistemological structure of the Christian faith'?"

Answer: Simply stated, it is both the explicit and tacit interpretation of the nature of knowledge according to the teaching of the Bible. It embraces the following questions: Can we know anything? If so, what can we know? How can we know? What are the limits of our knowledge? What is reason? Faith? The relation between reason and faith? What knowledge claims does the Christian faith make—and on what basis? Is the Christian faith based on postulates or are there some things that are foundationally certain? If the Christian claims a distinctive kind of knowledge, how is that claim to be intellectually justified? What is the nature of the relationship between premises and conclusion in such a justificative process? Is the Christian faith ultimately based on (that is, justified in terms of) theological premises or nontheological premises? Is it justified by way of deduction or induction or some other means—perhaps a synthesis of inference and nondiscursiveness?

Generally, presuppositionists disavow the possibility of knowledge, that is, *episteme* (certainty) in contradistinction to *doxa* (opinion). All claims fall under the rubric of *faith*. Verificationists tend to make a radical disjunction between faith and knowledge, however, claiming the attainability of the latter. Which should the Christian accept? Or is there a third alternative? The answers given to these questions will indicate how one conceives the epistemological structure of the Christian faith. The basic question, then, is this: Is there a given epistemological structure that stands in judgment on all conceptions that fall short of it, and, if so, what is it?

Question 3
"Would you provide some examples of 'neutral criteria'?"

Answer: Some verificationists claim certain states of affairs as "neutral criteria," while other verificationists select different states of affairs. The following list, therefore, is not to be taken as exhaustive or as a repertory of neutral criteria agreed upon by all verificationists: the foundational principles and rules of logic, sensory objects, the universality of reasoning processes, scientific methodology, historical traces, and historiography.

Some or all of these are understood to be "neutral criteria" because they are neither derived from, nor do they antecedently support, any particular religious or philosophical perspective. Since they are universally accessible and can be apprehended without bias, they can serve as criteria by which various points of view are critically assessed. Of course, thoroughgoing presuppositionists categorically deny the possibility of apprehending any state of affairs in a purely objective way, that is, the doctrine of "immaculate perception" is a delusion. For every act of apprehension is an act of interpretation. All facts, therefore, are "interprefacts."

I maintain that this presuppositionist contention is self-defeating. Nevertheless, the naivete of some verificationist interpretations of neutral criteria is to be avoided, and a careful epistemology should provide the means for doing so.

Question 4
"Would you give an example of postulation and coherence—especially as they apply to presuppositionism?"

Answer: By "postulation" I mean the mere assumption that a state of affairs obtains. That is, if one postulates a state of affairs, he does not discover it, or know it, or deductively infer it. Basic postulates are theories that form the foundational point of reference for other components in a system or perspective. They cannot be proved or derived from anything else. The following are examples of basic postulates: Plato's theories of the Forms, the demiurge, and the preexistence of the soul; Plotinus's doctrine of the ineffability of the One and his theory that matter is evil; Whitehead's theory that process is ultimate; Bergson's theory of the *elan vital.*

Some Christian presuppositionists seem to interpret the basic principles of logic as postulates, and when they claim that one must begin with the presupposition that the Bible is true—and from which *everything* else must be justified—they are saying that the Christian faith itself is a postulate. Although soteriologically one is put in the Christian faith by sovereign grace, they contend that intellectually one becomes a Christian by an act of postulation.

Coherence is akin to logical consistency but it also transcends it. The following two statements, for example, are mutually consistent, but that they are mutually coherent is not evident: "The house is on a hill" and "The number 7 is greater than the number 4." An example of coherence would be the following: "The number 7 is greater than the number 4"; "The number 8 is greater than the number 7"; "Therefore, the number 8 is greater than the number 4."

In the strict sense, coherence is indicated by logical implication. In a broader sense, coherence involves not only the logical consecution of deduction but also of induction and contextual relevance. Some Christian presuppositionists have argued that the logical coherence of the Christian faith suffices to demonstrate that it is true. Others have contended that empirical factors must be included if the Christian faith is to be justified by an appeal to systematic consistency. This means that historical data and other sensory data must by synoptically integrated to show its coherence in a fashion that includes but surpasses rigorous logical consecution. Gordon Clark has given us a conspicuous example of an apologetic that stresses logical coherence, and Edward Carnell has provided a perspective that emphasizes multifaceted coherence.

Question 5
"What is the justificational regress?"

Answer: In any intellectual attempt to support a claim, one engages in a process of appealing to reasons—or supposed reasons—to establish the credibility or truth of his contention. By invoking more universal or less questionable assertions as the basis for his claim, he regresses, or goes back, to something more fundamental. And since his aim is to substantiate a proposition that is called into question, that procedure is what is called the justificational regress.

The point at issue is whether the regress is infinite—that is, must every claim be justified? Or can the regress come to a legitimate halt because there are some truths that are absolute and self-evident? If there are no such truths, then justification cannot succeed, for calling a halt at any point is purely arbitrary. And arbitrariness is the antithesis of justification. Thus either one must show that some truths are absolute and self-evident or concede the impossibility of justification. The consequence of the latter is the embracement of either radical skepticism or comprehensive fideism.

Question 6
"What does Bartley mean by the assertion that a position that cannot overcome fideism is unable to refute skepticism?"

Answer: As I have indicated in my response to the previous question, unless one can show that there is a nonarbitrary way to decide among competing starting points, fideism cannot be overcome. That is, one accepts a starting point or primordial assumption by sheer faith. No reasons can be given, because the proffering of a reason is an appeal to something else, which is the actual starting point. And for that starting point there is no reason. Since there is no reason for the ultimate reason or touchstone, one can only embrace it fideistically or irrationally (that is, without reason). But if that is so, one can ask, "Why embrace it at all?" That question is unanswerable, as we have seen. Therefore, judgment can be suspended without violating any canons of rationality. That is another way of saying that skepticism is irrefutable if one cannot show how fideism can be overcome.

Question 7
"What is an infinite regress and why can't it justify anything?"

Answer: In view of the foregoing comments, a brief word should suffice here. An infinite regress must be understood to be infinite only in principle. For instance, if one says that every proposition must be justified in terms of another proposition, he has implicitly committed himself to an infinite regress. There could never be an end to such a process. And without an end, there is no justification—nothing can be appealed to as the final, absolute, indubitable touchstone.

Question 8
"Contra Popper, how can there be any refutation, much less an endless process of refutation, if there are no absolute criteria?"

Answer: Strictly speaking, for Popper there cannot be any refutation, and that is one important reason why his epistemology is unacceptable. To refute—in contradistinction to rejecting or attempting to disprove—is to show the falsity of a claim or position. One cannot show that a proposition is false or that an argument is invalid unless there are absolute criteria. For only if the criteria that are violated are certain can one say that a claim is refuted. Curiously enough, Popper recognizes this but repudiates it. It is his admission of this state of affairs that leads him to say that no "refutation" is certain or final. There is always the possibility that a new argument or new evidence will turn up that will serve to refute the refutation. And, in turn, that refutation is susceptible to refutation, *ad infinitum.*

In a sense, Popper wants to have it both ways. He wants refutation but he wants to reinterpret the nature of refutation so he can preserve skepticism and open-ended criticism. This semantic sleight of hand only tends to confuse. The choice of a term other than *refutation* would have been preferable. When he uses the term, then, he means that a claim is provisionally or tentatively believed to be false because of some negative considerations. When I use the term, however, I mean that a claim is false because it has been shown to be false by sufficient reasons.

The conclusiveness of refutation means that great caution should be exercised in remanding specific propositions to the category of the refuted. There is a great difference between refutation and problematicity, or between refutation and merely having evidence or reasons that count against, or between refutation and a mere denial that a claim is true or justifiable. But with due care, one can discriminate between these and avoid many premature judgments about the status of a claim. Only in this way, however, can one avoid the self-defeating assertions of Popper and Bartley, and only in this way can one have a sound epistemology. If one cannot categorically refute anything, he cannot know that any proposition is true, for one is the converse of the other.

Question 9
"Why, precisely, does Bartley say that a Christian, like every other non-Popperian, is an irrationalist?"

Answer: Bartley was misled by the false dilemma that either one must have a criterion of truth or he must be a skeptic. The quest for a criterion of truth he understood as a search for a point of reference outside every truth-claim and outside every state of affairs under consideration. In other words, the criterion by which *A* is appraised is *B,* and the criterion by which *B* is appraised is *C*, and so on. *This kind of criteriological pursuit is a chimera*, and anyone who embarks on it will most likely find himself a skeptic or a fideist. For he will eventually see that every criterion must itself have a criterion, *ad infinitum*.

Bartley is convinced that there are no authorities—that neither reason nor the senses are indubitable. Every alleged source of knowledge, every starting point, every criterion is open to refutation. For every thesis propounded by a philosopher, another thinker has advocated its contrary or contradictory. Universal agreement is unachievable because no position is sacrosanct. The only sensible attitude in this situation, according to Bartley, is to refrain from dogmatism and commitment. The history of philosophy is replete with instances of unexpected refutations. To hold any position with a dogmatic attitude or irrevocable commitment is to be an irrationalist, for it is going against reason—which must be understood not as an appeal to authorities but as open-ended criticism. Christianity requires commitment, and commitment is incompatible with open-ended criticism.

Bartley has done what a number of other thinkers have done, namely, defined reason in such biased fashion that Christianity must be irrational. The problem, of course, is with his arbitrary definition of reason—a definition, by the way, that leads to absurdities in his own position. Not only is there no good reason to accept his theory, therefore, but there are good reasons to reject it—primarily its inevitable entailment of logical contradiction.

Question 10
"Would you elaborate on the nature of the incoherence you perceive in nonjustificationalism?"

Answer: I develop my criticisms in detail in my forthcoming book, *Metapologetics: Can the Christian Faith be Justified?* The essential incoherence of nonjustificationalism can be stated succinctly, however. According to Bartley, literally every statement and procedure is open to refutation. This means that the principles and rules of logic are refutable. But refutation is the utilization of logical principles and rules to show that a theory, or statement, or position is false—at least "provisionally false." One does not have to show how logic can be refuted—which is impossible in any case—to exhibit the incoherency. One merely needs to conceive of the attempt to refute logic. Since there is no refutation without logic, logic must be acknowledged and implemented to attempt to refute logic. But every such attempt to refute logic obliquely concedes the irrefutability of logic. For if logic succeeded in refuting logic, either the refutation would be specious—for it must be based on logic—or the purported refutation would be logically unintelligible.

There is no way to escape the horns of this dilemma. The employment of logic in the attempt to refute logic is an implicit acknowledgement of the certainty and absoluteness of logic. There are some things (such as the principle of noncontradiction) that cannot be refuted—and are not even open to the possibility of refutation—because they are the necessary condition of *every* instance of attempted refutation.

Thus, Bartley's alleged position is not a genuine position, for it fails to achieve the self-consistency that is essential for every authentic theory. By rigorously following through with the foundational principles of nonjustificationalism, one can show that it reduces to absurdity.

Question 11
"Why is justification necessary in every promulgation of a truth claim?"

Answer: It is necessary simply because human beings are under rationality norms. That is, an utterance or the collection of marks on a page cannot be ascertained to be a truth claim unless certain canons of logic and language are complied with or implicitly apprehended. A statement must be well-formed if it is to communicate a propositional meaning—which alone is capable of being true or false, in the proper sense of those terms. To be true, a statement must conform to certain standards of intelligibility—namely, logical, semantic, contextual, and categorial (for instance, the statement, "The number 4 is yellow" violates the categorial norm). Implicit in every assertion of a truth claim, then, is an appeal to various norms of intelligibility. They are bases for justifying the meaning and coherence of what is being asserted.

It is also a rationality norm that dictates that there ought to be reasons for believing claims anyone makes. Even Bartley tacitly bowed to rationality norms when he wrote so he could be understood, and when he elaborately argued his thesis in a book that presented the alleged reasons for being a nonjustificationalist (his fundamental claim being that nonjustificationalism alone is *consistent* with all that we "know" about the history of philosophy and science).

Spouting statements in an intellectual vacuum is hardly the same as making truth-claims. Making a truth-claim carries the contextual implication that there are reasons for it—good reasons, connected with history, science, experimentation, observation, and so on. That is what it means to say that justification is necessary in every statement of a truth claim. No philosopher or scientist has ever been able to dispense with it.

Question 12
"What is a universal given?"

Answer: A universal given is a state of affairs (which may be anything—psychological, sensory, ideal, spiritual, or a combination of any of these) that is directly apprehensible, in principle, at all times and places. Although there are conditions for actually apprehending universal givens, they need not be apprehended by any particular individual in order to qualify them as universal. Sensory objects, for example, are universal givens, but if the colors of sensory objects are to be apprehended, one must have the means (functioning eyes, optical nerves, etc.) to do so.

The particular taste that I have in my mouth right now, or the particular emotion I feel at this moment is not a universal given as such but a special given. That is, it is presented to my consciousness directly and is not arrived at in some inferential manner. Nor is it something I postulate. What is given cannot be postulated. It may erroneously be thought to be postulated or it may wrongly be called a postulate.

Literally anything that can be veridically, nonpostulationally, and nondiscursively grasped by consciousness is a given. And if it is susceptible of apprehension by all human beings in principle, it is a universal given.

Question 13

"How can you show that every position explicitly or implicitly acknowledges certain universal givens? What if others deny your 'universal givens' or consider them hypotheses or postulates rather than givens?"

Answer: These are critical and important questions and they take us to the heart of veridicalism. The first question has already been answered in part. Rationality norms are universal givens that are integral to every position, for even if a position itself is wrong, it cannot be stated or formulated without some conformity to these canons. Even the denial of the principle of noncontradiction requires the principle itself, for no affirmation or denial can be made without conformity to the principle of noncontradiction. In fact, every position at least tacitly acknowledges psychological, sensory, and ideal states of affairs and the categorial differences among them. That this is so despite denials can be shown by an analysis of the claims that constitute any position, philosophical, religious, or otherwise. If rationality norms are flouted, no position can be conceived or stated, for there would be no unequivocal meanings. If categorial states of affairs are denied, they must first be grasped in order to be denied. This apprehension itself shows that one cannot dispense with universal givens.

The second question requires a clear grasp of the differences between logic and psychology, and between meaning and language. Merely affirming something does not make it so; neither does denial make it not so. Labeling a given a postulate is a category mistake no less than calling a number a sensory object. The way to discriminate between a given and a postulate or hypothesis is twofold: first, by bringing the state of affairs in question to adequate reflective scrutiny so that its qualities and structure are disclosed in their intrinsic lucidity, and, second, by analytical examination that determines its congruity with already-ascertained universal givens.

To be sure, these procedures are highly demanding in terms of rigor and critical analysis. And it is likely that some states of affairs will yield very slowly—and perhaps not at all—to unproblematic clarity. But that does not mean that there are not some clear cases. And that is all one needs to show the distinction between givens and postulates. That there is a difference is indicated by the unequivocal impossibility of postulating anything without a prior apprehension of meaning and elementary logical principles. Since the latter are always prior, as the necessary condition, to every act of postulation, they themselves cannot be postulated. A book entitled, *The Appeal to the Given*, by J. J. Ross, is a clear example of the denial of givens on the basis of the apprehension of givens.

Let me reemphasize a crucial observation: *If there are no givens, there can be no postulates.* Without them, there can be no theorizing or hypothesizing. This is too often forgotten, or never understood in the first place. Every denial of givenness is as self-defeating as every denial of the principle of noncontradiction. Once the inescapability of givenness is comprehended, the important question becomes: What kind of a given is state of affairs S—universal or special? Unless some states of affairs are given, no one can deny givenness or even call it into question. To put it differently, no denial or doubt would be possible without the givenness of certain states of affairs that make it possible to deny or doubt anything.

Question 14
"What is meant by reflective corroboration of a given's authenticity?"

Answer: Since a given cannot be arrived at discursively—that is, by inference from something else—how does one justify the claim that it is apprehended veridically? Justification cannot be carried out by showing deductive validity or inductive soundness. That which is nonderivative must be justified in some other way. The method is twofold. First, every step must be taken to insure that the object or state of affairs in question is brought before one's consciousness by direct apprehension. If it is claimed that a particular rose has a sweet fragrance, one can ascertain that it has by fulfilling the conditions essential for making it an object of direct awareness, that is, by smelling it under optimal or adequate conditions—both in the perceiver and the environment. Merely theorizing about the rose or inferring that it must have a sweet fragrance because other roses in the past have been so characterized falls short of the certainty provided by direct apprehension.

Second, since certitude (psychological assurance) has not infrequently been confused with certainty (objective apprehension), reflective corroboration may be necessary—not as a basis for inferring the state of affairs under consideration but as a way of checking its comportation with other givens. Moreover, the process of reflective corroboration may contribute to the conditions that occasion the direct apprehension of the state of affairs. But its primary function remains that of exhibiting the logical unity that obtains among true propositions.

A perspective that claims veridical givenness—as Mormonism, for example, speaks about "the burning in the bosom" as the final guarantee to the adherent that his religion is true—but whose tenets are mutually inconsistent cannot be true. Its devotees misconstrue their certitude as certainty that their religion is true. Since the universal givenness of the foundational principle of noncontradiction is violated by Mormonism's claim that it is the restoration of pristine Christianity and that the Bible, the Book of Mormon, the Doctrine and the Covenants, and the Pearl of Great Price are all revelations from God, the intensity of the subjective assurance that its adherents experience can never close the gap between certitude and certainty. Neither Mormonism nor any

other religious or philosophical perspective that entails fundamental contradictions can be true. And nothing that is false can
be veridically apprehended as true, no matter how profound the
feeling or desire that it be so.

Question 15
"What is veridical apprehension and what does it mean
to show congruence with universal givens?"

Answer: Our consciousness is presented with a vast ar-
ray of givens every day, and relatively few of them are called into
question. That is, in most cases there is no reason to question the
veridicality of the apprehension. An example or two will help to
elucidate the meaning of this. If one is aware of the dangers of
perceptual distortion because of subjective or environmental factors, such as a mirage in the desert, he is likely to be critically
skeptical of his apprehension. Taking a mirage to be extrasubjective sensory reality is to apprehend it nonveridically. Taking a
round penny to be elliptical because the angle of perception is
ignored is to apprehend it nonveridically.
   Veridical apprehension is the grasping by consciousness of a
state of affairs in terms of its intrinsic or objective features. The
terms *apprehension* and *grasping* are metaphors, but they are
vivid indicators of an act of consciousness—not unlike the use of
see to refer to an act of understanding or discernment. One cannot
be conscious without experiencing some apprehensions, and each
apprehension is either veridical or nonveridical. That is, a state
of affairs is grasped as it is in terms of its structure and qualities
or it is not so grasped.
   Let us suppose that the apprehension of a state of affairs or
some of its features is problematic—in the sense that whether it
is veridical or nonveridical is difficult to determine. If it is veridical, the authenticity of the apprehension will be corroborated
by showing its agreement with, and support from, other universal
givens. If there is incompatibility, logical or ontological, between
the alleged deliverances of the apprehension and other givens
whose status is not open to question (e.g., the principle of non-

contradiction), the claim of veridicality is undermined. In some instances, such a determination is fairly simple. In others, it is extremely complex. Some claims are contrary to evidence, others are devoid of all evidence, and still others are devoid of sufficient evidence. The most difficult determination is generally the last one, that is, ascertaining the adequacy of the evidence. In spite of enormously complex issues that plague theories of probability, in some sense a distinction must be made between the probable and the improbable, and between degrees of probability. Not everything is susceptible of the clear-cut precision of arithmetic. Nevertheless, rationality norms are sufficiently comprehensive to embrace many other dimensions of thought and life. Problematic cases notwithstanding, some verdicts in a court of law are clearly established beyond any reasonable doubt.

The relation between a given and the evidence that corroborates its apprehension is crucial to the distinctiveness of veridicalism. The foundational realities of the Christian faith are not discursively arrived at by beginning with extra-Christian or non-theological data or premises. The claim that they are is an interpretation of the relation which constitutes the essence of verificationism. Nor are the foundational Christian realities postulated and made the determinants for interpreting all data. The claim that they are is a view of the relation which constitutes the essence of presuppositionism. Rather, according to veridicalism, foundational Christian realities are givens—and, therefore, directly apprehensible—and other data and argumentation are corroborative of the apprehension. To emphasize the critical point again—such data and argumentation are not the source or the premises for arriving at the essential realities of the Christian faith. According to veridicalism, there are two inseparable dimensions to the justification of the truth claims of the Christian faith. On the one hand, its foundational realities must be grasped veridically and nondiscursively in the context of cognitively apprehended meanings, that is, the message of the gospel (I Cor. 15:1-4; Rom. 1:16). By reflection on the object and content of the apprehension to determine the veridicality of the act, one fulfills the first dimension of the justificational process. For example, if the gospel is misunderstood as a message of legalism (Gal. 1:6-9), its efficacy and purpose are frustrated in the life of the individual who misapprehends it (Gal. 2:21; II Cor. 13:5; I Cor. 15:13-17).

The second dimension of the justificational process is fulfilled when one thoroughly traces the significance and implications of the Christian faith relative to the whole of thought and life to show that they are consonant with universal givens and the propositions that are soundly derived from them. This involves a broad spectrum of logical and empirical factors. Degrees of relevance obviously vary, but nothing is to be antecedently excluded or distorted in favor of the justificandum (that which is to be justified). Religious and philosophical views frequently succumb to this temptation. Indeed, presuppositionism is especially vitiated by such a bias. But no one, irrespective of his method or perspective, is automatically exempt from this fallacy, and if rationality norms are to be respected, one must be on guard in all of his reasoning processes.

Whatever the reasons or causes, an individual may find that what he has taken to be a veridical apprehension he now calls into question. Or his claim to a veridical apprehension may be challenged by someone else. In such circumstances, a rationally concerned person pursues the justificational process. If this is done properly, and with sufficient rigor and responsiveness to rationality norms, the nature of the apprehension in question will either be disclosed as veridical or nonveridical—or, in some cases, problematic.

It cannot be overstressed that the justificatory process must include both dimensions indicated above. To use an analogy, justifying the claim that a particular rose has a sweet fragrance is not accomplished merely by showing that the claim in no way violates rationality norms and in every way comports with all relevant considerations. If one can, he ought to smell the rose. As Edmund Husserl used to emphasize: go to the things themselves.

Nevertheless, having gone to the thing itself, one does not fulfill the conditions of justification in their entirety, for he must add to direct apprehension a demonstration of its congruity with all relevant givens and their legitimate implications. If something on my upper lip, and not the rose, is the source of the sweet fragrance I smell, careful analysis and rigorous experimentation are likely to reveal it.

Concern for veridicality of apprehension, particularly with reference to the most important dimensions of human existence, ought to characterize every human being. That is another way of saying that the question of truth is the most important question human beings can raise. And the more ultimate the issue, the more urgent the question. Unfortunately, most members of mankind seem to be more interested in other considerations and tend to value group loyalty and emotional and temporal advantage above truth.

Question 16
"What is the difference between the special givens of the Christian faith and the universal givens of rational experience?"

Answer: The basic difference is that the former are unavailable apart from the cognitive content of the gospel and the work of the Holy Spirit. This does not mean that God's reality is known only on these two bases. Knowing the reality of God should not be confused with knowing God. All human beings have an awareness of God's reality (Rom. 1:18-20). Only some human beings—those who come to Christ in faith, genuinely believing the gospel—know God (Matt. 11:27; John 14:6). Awareness of God's reality, which provides a basis for our responsibility to Him, is a universal experience, and God's reality is a universal given.

Knowing God, in contrast to being aware of God's reality, is a special given of the Christian faith, and the special experience of those who trust Christ. The Bible is also a special given. As a mere empirical object it is a universal given, that is, a sensory object accessible, in principle, to anyone. But as the message of God, it is a special given. To take it as a merely human product is to apprehend it nonveridically. But to accept it "not as the word of men, but as it actually is, the word of God" (I Thess. 2:13) is to apprehend it veridically. As such, it is a special given. And so it is with regeneration and the indwelling of the Holy Spirit. None of these special givens can be experientially apprehended apart from basic cognitive content (Matt. 13:23; I John 2:23). This is in sharp contrast to experientialism, the view that "religious experience" is ineffable. The limitations and incoherencies of experientialism are well known to most philosophers and apologists.

Although the fundamental difference between universal givens and the special givens of the Christian faith is their *natural* availability and unavailability, respectively, crucial similarities between them obtain as well. For instance, neither universal nor special givens can be discursively derived from something else. They are only known by direct apprehension, and the veridicality of the apprehension is justified by both reflection and corroboration.

One cannot discursively prove the existence of extrasubjective sensory objects, for example. These universal givens are directly apprehended by means of certain physiological and environmental conditions. They are not postulated or inferred. But that certain perceptual objects are veridically grasped can be corroborated—by invoking more than one of the senses, by arguing inductively from the perceptual experience of others, by experimentation on the sensory objects in question, and so forth. None of these—singly or in combination—will suffice as the premises for an argument to prove the existence of sensory objects. Indeed, such an argument would be circular. The certainty with which we apprehend sensory objects also transcends the probability of inductive arguments. In fact, no argument can ever be originative but only corroborative of the veridicality of our awareness of sensory objects.

The same epistemological structure characterizes one's knowledge of his own self, knowledge of basic logical principles, and so forth. These givens cannot be proved from other data or premises. They are first directly grasped and then, by extending the process of critical reflection, they are corroborated by relevant lines of evidence and argumentation. This is also the case with the universal given of God's reality and with the special givens of the Christian faith. This means that one does not begin with nontheological premises—as is the procedure of the classical theistic arguments—to arrive at a proof for the existence of God. The nondiscursive awareness of God's reality can be corroborated, however, by numerous lines of substantiation. The same holds for the Christian faith itself, and therefore it has the same justificational structure as general epistemology and the most fundamental certainties of human experience.

Question 17

"In what sense do presuppositionists claim that their position alone is adequate to epistemological and biblical data?"

Answer: In general, presuppositionists maintain that all "knowledge" is based on faith; since one can never prove or justify his basic premises, he must presuppose them or view them as assumptions. Since everyone is under the same limitation, the presuppositionist claims that he is entitled to begin with Christian assumptions. He also insists that in doing so consciously, he is more critical than those who imperceptively think of their starting points as obvious, apodictic, or proven truths.

The presuppositionist finds putative support for his perspective in a variety of biblical passages, most notably Hebrews 11:6— he who comes to God must *believe* that God exists. This negates the legitimacy of attempted theistic proofs. Indeed, the entire Bible is said to "assume" the existence of God. In this way the presuppositionist holds that his approach provides the only adequate apologetic for the Christian faith, for it alone conforms to the structure of general epistemology and to the priority of faith laid down to biblical teaching.

Question 18

"How is 'adequacy' applied as a universal justificational norm?"

Answer: Whatever a theory may be—and in whatever field of inquiry—there is an implicit claim that it adequately,

even if provisionally, interprets a state of affairs. Presuppositionists seek to justify their procedure on the basis of a general appeal
to epistemology and a specific appeal to the Bible, as we have
seen in connection with question 17. When presuppositionists do
this, they are implicitly acknowledging "adequacy" as a given.
Their starting point, therefore, is not the Bible or the Christian
faith, as they aver, but the principle of adequacy. They must either
relinquish presuppositionism by admitting that there are givens—
even if this is the only one—or they must maintain that the
principle of adequacy is itself a postulate. If they opt for the latter
alternative, they must admit that their acquiescence to the principle as a criterion is arbitrary, and there is no more justification
for adopting it than there is for rejecting it.

If a presuppositionist says that he adopts his starting point
because it is useful or fruitful, he merely recasts the problem in
terms of another principle. In the final analysis, a presuppositionist cannot retain his epistemological identity if he claims any
nonarbitrariness in the choice of his foundational premises. For
to be nonarbitrary is to have some reason for choosing one premise rather than another. This will lead either to the recognition of
givenness, thereby destroying comprehensive presuppositionism,
or to a construal of reasons as purely arbitrary, thereby precluding
the possibility of justification at all. In any case, every attempt to
present a theoretical perspective—whether religious or philosophical or whatever—inescapably, if tacitly, implies that a *principle of adequacy* (that the theory is adequate to the problem, the
data, the evidence, the arguments, etc.) justifies it. It thus functions as a rationality norm, and that is what it means to be a
universal justificational standard.

Question 19
"What is the difference between truth and validity, and
how does the difference between them apply to an appraisal of metaphysical positions?"

Answer: There are only two truth-values: truth and falsity. These values apply only to propositions, that is, the *meaning*

expressed by declarative sentences or sentences that can be legitimately transformed into declarative sentences. In logic, validity applies only to deductive arguments, consisting of two or more propositions, one of which is claimed to follow necessarily from the other(s). Every such argument is either valid or invalid. If the propositions which constitute the argument are true, and the conclusion follows necessarily from the premises, the argument is sound.

By analogy, a metaphysical position is like a vast argument, although it usually encompasses much more than deduction. Nonetheless, even if it is characterized by one correct logical consecution after another so that the entirety constitutes a complex valid argument, the metaphysical position cannot be considered the truth about reality. One can have logical coherence without true propositions. One must ask about the truth-value of each of the constitutive tenets of the metaphysical perspective.

Assuming, for example, that there are only twenty known metaphysical perspectives, we are not entitled to say that since nineteen of them are unsound due to inherent contradictions or false tenets, the twentieth must be true, even if it is a piece of valid reasoning. There may be metaphysical positions "twenty-one," "twenty-two," and so on, that may be characterized by valid logical consecution. Validity alone cannot guarantee the truth of any argument's propositions.

Similarly, the truth of the premises of an argument is not sufficient to guarantee the validity of the argument. All the propositions of a valid argument may be false and all the propositions of an invalid argument may be true. The following is an example of the former: "All human beings have six legs; the Statue of Liberty is a human being; therefore, the Statue of Liberty has six legs." The argument is valid but unsound. An example of an invalid argument with true propositions is the following: "Nuts are good for some people; some people eat nuts; therefore, some people do good things for other people."

Comprehensive interpretations of reality (i.e., metaphysical perspectives) are not rationally credible if they encompass basic contradictions and invalid inferences or if they are fundamentally constituted by false tenets. Formal validity and material truth are both essential for a sound perspective.

Question 20
"What is the difference between the logical and ontological principles of noncontradiction?"

Answer: The logical principle applies to propositions. It asserts that a proposition cannot be both true and not true. The ontological principle applies to nonpropositional states of affairs. It asserts that something (a state of affairs or object) cannot both be and not be in the same respect. Since every proposition refers to a state of affairs, the principles are inseparable counterparts. A proposition cannot be true and false, because the state of affairs to which it refers cannot both be and not be in the same sense.

Question 21
"What is the law of parsimony?"

Answer: This principle is usually credited to William of Occam, who in the fourteenth century stated: "Entities should not be multiplied beyond necessity." It is the ideal of simplicity that generally prevails in the sciences. It is assumed that the fewer the number of hypotheses or categories that are used for explaining a set of phenomena, the better the theory. Of course, this guideline has its dangers, and someone has pejoratively referred to Occam's razor as "Occam's eraser." Reality may not be as simple as we assume or desire. It is better to have complexity with truth than simplicity with falsehood. The latter error is known as *reductionism*, the attempt to explain one kind of reality in terms of another when there is an ontological or qualitative hiatus between them (for example, materialism in ontology and behaviorism in psychology are justifiably charged with committing the error of reductionism).

Question 22
"What are some of the epistemological and metaphysical presuppositions that are mutually implicit in one another

and serve to make them inseparable although distinguishable?"

Answer: As a theory of reality, metaphysics must locate knowledge somewhere on its interpretive map. Obviously, in that sense, they are inseparable. Moreover, one cannot have a theory of knowledge without asking what kinds of things we know, and one cannot have a theory of reality without asking how reality is known. To know or believe is to know or believe *something*. Every proposition refers to some state of affairs, and reality consists of states of affairs—whatever their nature may be. Different kinds of realities, such as are described in what is called "regional ontology," may be known in different ways or by different means.

Reality appears to be complex. Ways of knowing also appear to be complex. But neither one can be adequately understood without analyzing both—at least in terms of a descriptive metaphysics that examines things that present themselves to our consciousness. Going beyond that kind of metaphysics is what is known as "revisionary metaphysics," an interpretation of reality in terms of that which is not directly presented to consciousness but is postulated or speculatively inferred. But whatever type of metaphysics one seeks to formulate, some epistemological questions must be answered, either explicitly or implicitly. The same holds for the converse.

Question 23
"Would you elaborate on the *petitio principii* committed by limited verificationism?"

Answer: In order to use nontheological premises to inductively justify the Christian faith, limited verificationism must interpret its premises within the framework of Christian tenets. Since it is possible to interpret data from the standpoint of different metaphysical perspectives, an atheistic or materialistic ontology would preclude the methods and content of limited verificationism's starting points from ever arriving at the probabilification of the Christian faith—or, for that matter, providing it with any support whatever. Since limited verificationism contends that such starting points guarantee the assertion of the probability of the Christian faith, it must smuggle in Christian premises at the outset.

Immanuel Kant's approach, to use an analogy, exemplified the impossibility of doing what the limited verificationist purports to accomplish. Kant's ethical premises did not contain theological tenets. Consequently, he rightly spoke of his inference that God exists as a postulate of faith, not an inductive or deductive conclusion. Either the verificationist's Christian-theistic conclusion is a postulate or it is already surreptitiously concealed in the premises. If it is the former, the verificationist is actually a presuppositionist. If it is the latter, the verificationist has begged the question by circular reasoning.

Question 24
"Would you more fully explain the five starting points distinguished by veridicalism?"

Answer:
(1) The ontological starting point is the Triune God, for all of reality is dependent upon God who is the sole, eternal Creator. There is no eternal reality apart from God or above God. God does not come to be, nor is he derived from anything else. It is in this sense that he alone is the ontological starting point.

(2) The epistemological starting point is that which is primordial in the knowing process. The possibility and nature of human knowing is rooted in the *imago Dei*, and this makes man's cognitive experience unique among all the creatures on earth. The vitiating effects of sin must also be considered as a factor in the distinctiveness of human knowing and its limitations. Nevertheless, we have no other starting point for knowledge than our own consciousness. That is not to say that consciousness is the source or that it is self-sufficient, for there would be no knowledge without input from other sources. And there would be no spiritual knowledge without divine revelation—general and special. But

there can be no knowledge without consciousness, and in that sense consciousness is the basis or starting point of knowledge.

(3) The justificational starting point is the frame of reference for showing the rational credibility of the Christian faith. Veridicalism maintains that *both* the constitutive doctrines of the Christian faith and universal givens form a complex starting point. This is in fundamental contrast to presuppositionism, which begins with the former alone, and verificationism, which begins with the latter alone. Of course, beginning with the special givens of the Christian faith does not mean that one has already assumed what is to be justified. Rather, if one is raising the question of *justification*, he begins with them as problematic content whose veridicality or nonveridicality is to be ascertained by showing their isomorphism or continuity with epistemology in general and with other relevant givens in particular.

(4) The interpretive starting point is that metaphysical framework in which all else is to be explained and evaluated. The ontological perspective of the Christian faith—having been apprehended by human cognitive powers under the illuminating work of the Holy Spirit, and having been justified by the apologetics of veridicalism—is the touchstone for the general mapping of every object and every state of affairs in the scheme of things.

(5) The methodological starting point for the purposes of applied apologetics is variable because it is always the specific situation of the person or society being addressed with the gospel. Accordingly, the Christian apologist seeks to discover existential concerns and felt questions so that he can develop his case for the gospel by showing its relevance to the people he seeks to convince.

Each starting point answers a different question: (1) Ontological: What is the ultimate reality? (2) Epistemological: How do we know? (3) Justificational: What are the rational grounds for the truth-claims of the Christian faith? (4) Interpretive: How are we to determine the meaning and value of the welter of entities and states of affairs in the world? (5) Methodological: What should determine the specific approach of a Christian apologist in his endeavor to convincingly relate the gospel of Christ to people?

Question 25
"Would you amplify the significance of the four major categories of presuppositions?"

Answer: Both presuppositionism and verificationism fail to distinguish these radically different meanings of "presupposition." Just as much of the progress of the various intellectual disciplines has been due to the making of increasingly adequate distinctions—where only a few or perhaps none had been previously recognized—so in the area of apologetics, disclosing the variety of meanings that lurk in the usage of "presupposition" and other crucial terms is a key factor in achieving a viable methodology.

For many thinkers the term *presupposition* seems to have only one meaning, namely, a faith-postulate or unprovable assumption. But for the sake of semantic clarity or for the purpose of propositional justification what one explicitly or tacitly presupposes may belong to any one of a variety of categories. In a very real sense, for example, the apprehension or expression of any meaning depends upon or presupposes the principle of noncontradiction. Nevertheless, the latter principle is not a postulate whose truth-value is problematic. It is a universal given and it is true; otherwise, nothing could be true or could even be postulated.

By "systematic postulate" I mean a presupposition whose truth-value is unknown. It is assumed by an act of creative imagination or speculative inference as a basis for formulating an interpretive perspective. As such, it functions as a foundational theory that shapes the structure and significance of the entire system. The axioms of geometry are currently understood to have such a status and function. Every metaphysical philosophy has one or more postulates of this sort. The other propositions of the system depend upon them in one way or another, and, therefore, they are presupposed by them.

"Heuristic hypotheses" are not propounded as foundation pillars for a system but as imaginative guesses to serve methodological purposes. They constitute a crucial part of the empirical sciences, for they are part of our attempt to make sense out of data. They are formulated as conjectures so they can be tested in an attempt to determine their truth or falsity. In this way they help us to discover or investigate the world and its features.

"Forensic assumptions" are propositions that are stipulated in order to show consecutional relations between them and other propositions that are inferred from them. For instance, suppose a logic professor says to his students: "Let's assume that manlike beings have come to earth from Andromeda, taking only two days to get here. It follows that they had to travel at a rate that exceeded the speed of sound." He does not assert that such aliens have actually come to earth. As a presupposition for inferring the conclusion, the premise is a forensic assumption—and may be employed for purely pedagogical reasons.

Only by discriminating between presuppositions that are givens and presuppositions that are postulates, either problematic or patently false, can the possibility—indeed, the necessity—of veridicalism be understood. If there is even one given—and I have sought to show that there is (specifically, the principle of noncontradiction)—presuppositionism is untenable.

Question 26
"What does it mean for universal awareness of God to be mediated nondiscursively?"

Answer: Romans 1:18-20 asserts that human beings are conscious of God's reality in conjunction with their awareness of the created order. But it does not teach that such awareness is the consequence of an argument (that is, discursiveness). Attempts to justify the use of cosmological and teleological arguments on the basis of this passage are gratuitous. No inferential process is indicated. But neither is God's reality apprehended in a vacuum. Rather, such awareness is experienced as the created order, including one's own being, is reflectively apprehended. Thus, God's reality is mediated to our consciousness noninferentially.

In analogous fashion, I am conscious of the reality of my *self* (in contradistinction to my body) and I am aware of sensory objects. I do not know these realities by inference. However, I do not know them apart from the mediating function of other objects—in the former case, the contents of consciousness, and in the latter case, the neurological system and environmental conditions. Our knowledge of God's reality is both direct and certain, although conveyed to us by means of the created order.

Question 27
"Why can't one know the self's reality inferentially?"

Answer: In order to infer the reality of the self, the premises from which the inference is made must already refer to the self. And for such reference to be made, there must be a prior awareness of the self. Any argument that purports to prove the existence of the self must therefore be circular. Descartes's famous *cogito* argument exemplifies this error. The reason that he could infer "I exist" is because the existence of the "I" was already implicit in the premise, "I think," and the unexpressed premise, "There is no thinking without personal existence." Descartes failed to recognize that his argument was indicative of the noninferential grasp of the self's reality and that this direct apprehension yielded the certainty that could not be achieved by any inferential process. To sum up the point, we cannot know the self's reality inferentially because the inference presupposes a prior knowledge of the self. One cannot begin with the totally nonself and derive the self from it.

Question 28
"Is your approach (veridicalism) question-begging because you appeal to biblical material?"

Answer: No, because veridicalism is a comprehensive term embracing both metapologetics and apologetics, and as such, it *must* make use of biblical data. Metapologetics is directed primarily to Christians, and they do not need to be convinced of the truth-claims of the Christian faith. Its aim is to show how to justify the Christian faith, not to present the justification for the Christian faith. The latter is the province of apologetics proper.

As a Christian, one cannot do justice to the metapologetic question without recourse and subservience to biblical teaching. If apologetics, which is directed to the non-Christian, proceeds on the assumption that the Bible is true, it begs the question. And when that assumption is made, fideistic presuppositionism is the result, not veridicalism.

Question 29

"Would you restate how it is that veridicalism harmonizes self-evidence and discursive justification?"

Answer: This is the key issue in defining veridicalism. Presuppositionism and verificationism cannot be harmonized because they hold contradictory positions. In view of the inescapability of givens, however, veridicalism dispenses with the postulational foundation of presuppositionism and verificationism both—recall that verificationists interpret general epistemological principles and procedures fideistically. Universal givens are self-evidencing (but not verbally undeniable) to human beings with reflective capacity (that is, all human beings besides very young children and the mentally deranged or disordered). Taking this clue from epistemology and examining the Scriptures on this topic, veridicalism finds the special givens of the Christian faith inseparable from the universal givens of rational experience. The latter are not derived from the former—although they are just as dependent upon God as Creator and sustainer of all things—and, therefore, universal givens can function as relatively autonomous points of reference for corroboration. It must be stressed that they are corroborative in function, not originative or verificational. If they were originative, the Christian faith would be derivable from them—a radical natural theology that would virtually destroy the need for special revelation. If they were verificational, the Christian faith would be no more than a hypothesis that achieves some degree of confirmation—but always short of certainty. But since certainty is provided by veridical self-evidence, it can be attained by such an apprehension itself.

For purposes of justification, however, the corroboration that universal givens alone can provide is *necessary*. The principle of the unity of truth dictates that there must be agreement between authentic special givens and authentic universal givens, the latter supporting the former since it is the truth-value of the special givens that is in question. Of course, there may be situations in which they are not called into question, and in such a case they may be used to corroborate universal givens. Veridicalism harmonizes the self-evidence of both special and universal givens with discursive justification by showing how one category inferentially corroborates the other.

Question 30
"How can there be any univocity of knowledge common to God, who is infinite, and man, who is finite?"

Answer: The truth-value of a proposition is unchangeable, and the nature of the knower has no bearing on it. That is not to deny that there is an eternal and unbridgeable hiatus between the exhaustive knowledge that God has of everything and the nonexhaustive knowledge that characterizes the cognition of all of his creatures.

The truth or falsity of a proposition, if *known* by man at all, is known by God and man univocally. If this were not so, neither one would have knowledge. God knows all things, and he knows all propositions and whether they are true or false. Thus, if a proposition is true, God knows that it is true, and I can know it is true—if I am capable of knowing it at all—only on that basis. This is essentially what is meant by univocity of knowledge between God and man.

Any other position is self-defeating. For example, if such univocity were denied, then the denier must hold that the denial is true. And if it is true, God must know it to be true as well. But if both the human denier and God know it to be true, then there is some univocity of knowledge between God and man. Moreover, a denial of any univocity leads to the most radical theological agnosticism and destroys the credibility of the Scriptures.

Bibliography

Ayers, Robert H., and Blackstone, William T., eds. *Religious Language and Knowledge*. Athens: University of Georgia Press, 1972.

Barth, Karl. *Church Dogmatics*. Ed. G. W. Bromiley and Thomas F. Torrance. Edinburgh: T. and T. Clark, 1936-69.

Bartley, William W., III. *The Retreat to Commitment*. New York: Knopf, 1962.

Blanshard, Brand. *The Nature of Thought*. 2 vols. New York: Humanities Press, 1964.

Brown, Colin. *Philosophy and the Christian Faith*. London: Tyndale, 1968.

Bunge, Mario, ed. *The Critical Approach to Science and Philosophy*. New York: Free Press, 1964.

Carnell, Edward J. *An Introduction to Christian Apologetics*. Rev. ed. Grand Rapids: Eerdmans, 1955.

———. *A Philosophy of the Christian Religion*. Grand Rapids: Eerdmans, 1952.

Clark, Gordon H. *A Christian View of Men and Things*. Grand Rapids: Eerdmans, 1952.

———. *Karl Barth's Theological Method*. Nutley, N.J.: Presbyterian and Reformed, 1963.

———. *Religion, Reason, and Revelation*. Nutley, N.J.: Presbyterian and Reformed, 1961.

———. *Thales to Dewey*. Boston: Houghton Mifflin, 1957.

———. *Three Types of Religious Philosophy*. Nutley, N.J.: Craig Press, 1973.

Diamond, Malcolm L., and Litzenburg, Thomas V., Jr., eds. *The Logic of God: Theology and Verification*. Indianapolis: Bobbs-Merrill, 1975.

Dooyeweerd, Herman. *In the Twilight of Western Thought*. Nutley, N.J.: Craig Press, 1965.

Dowey, Edward A., Jr. *The Knowledge of God in Calvin's Theology*. New York: Columbia University Press, 1952.

Edwards, Paul, ed. *The Encyclopedia of Philosophy*. 8 vols. New York: Macmillan, 1967.

Edwards, Rem B. *Reason and Religion: An Introduction to the Philosophy of Religion*. New York: Harcourt Brace Jovanovich, 1972.

Flew, Antony. *God and Philosophy*. London: Hutchinson, 1966.

_____. *The Presumption of Atheism*. New York: Harper and Row, 1976.

_____, and MacIntyre, Alasdair, eds. *New Essays in Philosophical Theology*. New York: Macmillan, 1964.

Geehan, E. R., ed. *Jerusalem and Athens*. Nutley, N.J.: Presbyterian and Reformed, 1971.

Geisler, Norman. *Christian Apologetics*. Grand Rapids: Baker, 1976.

_____. *Philosophy of Religion*. Grand Rapids: Zondervan, 1974.

Gill, Jerry H. *The Possibility of Religious Knowledge*. Grand Rapids: Eerdmans, 1971.

Gollwitzer, Helmut. *The Existence of God as Confessed by Faith*. Philadelphia: Westminster Press, 1965.

Hamilton, Kenneth. *What's New in Religion?* Grand Rapids: Eerdmans, 1968.

Henry, Carl F. H., ed. *Christian Faith and Modern Theology*. New York: Channel Press, 1964.

_____, ed. *Contemporary Evangelical Thought*. New York: Harper, 1957.

_____. *God, Revelation and Authority*. 4 vols. to date.Waco, Tex.: Word, 1976–.

_____, ed. *Revelation and the Bible*. Grand Rapids: Baker, 1958.

Hick, John. *Arguments for the Existence of God*. New York: Seabury, 1971.

_____, ed. *Faith and the Philosophers*. New York: St. Martin's Press, 1966.

Holmes, Arthur F. *All Truth Is God's Truth*. Grand Rapids: Eerdmans, 1977.

_____. *Philosophy: A Christian Perspective*. Rev. ed. Chicago: InterVarsity Press, 1975.

Husserl, Edmund. *Logical Investigations*. Translated by J. N. Findlay. New York: Humanities Press, 1970.

Kuhn, Thomas S. *The Structure of Scientific Revolutions*. Second ed., enlarged. Chicago: University of Chicago Press, 1970.

Lewis, Gordon R. *Testing Christianity's Truth-Claims*. Chicago: Moody Press, 1976.

Mitchell, Basil, ed. *Faith and Logic*. London: Allen and Unwin, 1957.

_____. *The Justification of Religious Belief*. New York: Seabury, 1974.

_____, ed. *The Philosophy of Religion*. New York: Oxford University Press, 1971.

Montaigne, Michel de. *In Defense of Raymond Sebond.* Trans. A. H. Beattie. New York: Ungar, 1959.

Montgomery, John W. *The Shape of the Past.* Ann Arbor: Edwards Bros., 1968.

———. *Where is History Going?* Grand Rapids: Zondervan, 1969.

Nash, Ronald H., ed. *The Philosophy of Gordon Clark.* Philadelphia: Presbyterian and Reformed, 1968.

Pinnock, Clark. *Biblical Revelation.* Chicago: Moody Press, 1971.

Pivcevic, Edo, ed. *Phenomenology and Philosophical Understanding.* London: Cambridge University Press, 1975.

Plantinga, Alvin, ed. *Faith and Philosophy.* Grand Rapids: Eerdmans, 1964.

———. *God and Other Minds.* Ithaca, N.Y.: Cornell University Press, 1967.

———. *God, Freedom and Evil.* New York: Harper, 1974.

———. *The Ontological Argument.* Garden City, N.Y.: Doubleday, 1965.

Polanyi, Michael. *Personal Knowledge: Towards a Post-Critical Philosophy.* New York: Harper, 1964.

Popper, Karl R. *Conjectures and Refutations.* New York: Harper, 1968.

———. *The Logic of Scientific Discovery.* London: Hutchinson, 1959.

———. *Objective Knowledge.* London: Oxford University Press, 1972.

Quine, W. V. *From a Logical Point of View.* New York: Harper, 1963.

———, and Ullian, J. S. *The Web of Belief.* New York: Random House, 1970.

Ramm, Bernard. *The God Who Makes a Difference.* Waco, Tex.: Word, 1977.

———. *Types of Apologetic Systems.* Wheaton, Ill.: Van Kampen Press, 1953.

Reymond, Robert. *The Justification of Knowledge.* Philadelphia: Presbyterian and Reformed, 1976.

Ross, J. J. *The Appeal to the Given: A Study in Epistemology.* London: Allen and Unwin, 1970.

Torrance, Thomas F. *God and Rationality.* London: Oxford University Press, 1971.

Van Til, Cornelius. *The Case for Calvinism.* Philadelphia: Presbyterian and Reformed, 1964.

———. *A Christian Theory of Knowledge.* Philadelphia: Presbyterian and Reformed, 1969.

———. *The Defense of the Faith.* Philadelphia: Presbyterian and Reformed, 1969.

———. *The Great Debate Today.* Philadelphia: Presbyterian and Reformed, 1970.

Wittgenstein, Ludwig. *Philosophical Investigations.* Trans. G. E. M. Anscombe. New York: Macmillan, 1953.

Wolterstorff, Nicholas. *Reason Within the Bounds of Religion.* Grand Rapids: Eerdmans, 1976.

Zahrnt, Heinz. *The Question of God.* New York: Harcourt Brace Jovanovich, 1970.